FOREVER VILLA

by
David Instone

In Association With The
Birmingham Post & Mail

Thomas Publications

First published in Great Britain in September, 2005, by
Thomas Publications, PO Box 17, Newport,
Shropshire, England, TF10 7WT
www.thomaspublications.co.uk

ISBN 0 9550585 0 3

Printed and bound by Cromwell Press, Trowbridge

Contents

Introduction

Aston Villa are very much to the fore when it comes to English football clubs with proud histories. As founder members of the Football League, they are steeped in the traditions of the game and able to boast a long line of honours.

Which made them a natural choice as the subject for what is in effect a pictorial history; a history now stretching across one completed century and parts of two others.

Villa did plenty of trophy-gathering in the late 1800s but, in much more modern times, won the FA Cup at the expense of Manchester United in 1957 and, in the pre-Premiership era, lifted the League Championship under Ron Saunders in 1981 and then the European Cup under Tony Barton on that unforgettable evening in Rotterdam 12 months later.

Throw in the European Super Cup in 1983 and five League Cups in the 1960s, 1970s and 1990s - and it becomes a long story of memorable deeds that form the backbone of the tribute we have happily compiled in association with the Birmingham Post & Mail.

Forever Villa is, we believe, the biggest, best and most exclusive collection of action, celebration, dressing-room and boardroom photographs ever published about the club. Close on 400 pictures appear within the 192 pages of this book and, with around 150 goals captured, it's one sure to provoke many a happy memory for different generations to savour.

It's a walk down Memory Lane, a nostalgic trawl and the potential basis for lounge, bar-room or workplace discussion: Is it really that long ago since that match was played? Was he still playing then? And did they really wear shorts like that?

We have worked extremely diligently to avoid duplication of images from the many worthy previous books on the club. The odd picture might have slipped through the net but, by and large, we have done all we can to ensure that supporters will be flicking the pages within and feasting their eyes on hundreds of photos they haven't previously seen - at least not beyond collections of dusty old Sports Arguses, Sunday Mercurys, Birmingham Posts, Evening Mails and Evening Gazettes!

The sourcing of material has largely been done by us over numerous visits to Colmore Row but we couldn't have seen through this project without the generous assistance of our friends at the Post & Mail. The group continue to provide an essential day-to-day source of information for Villa fans far and wide but their extensive archive library is a treasure chest of memories and we're happy to report that, unlike many newspapers, they have resisted the urge to weed out old stock and bin it!

We would like to say a particular thank-you to Adam Fradgley, from the Post & Mail photographic department, for his embracing of an idea that we first mooted early in 2004. His encouragement and cooperation are much appreciated, as is his help in locating pictures from the electronic era of the last decade and a bit; the beginning of the end of hard-copy, tangible black and white pictures, sub-editors' markings and all!

The efforts of the Post & Mail's scanning department are also gratefully acknowledged, as is the assistance of the library staff whose job it is to keep good order in an Aladdin's Cave of a football archive. The Evening Mail and Villa themselves have also generously promoted the book in their columns and other media outlets and so helped more than 250 fans have their names in the scroll of honour at the back for posterity.

Last and definitely not least in the production phase of this book, we should pay tribute to the many fine Post & Mail photographers, past and present, whose keen eye and skills have captured so many famous, quirky and often forgotten moments for the masses to pore over. Rob Bishop, John Lalley and the author's wife, Liz, have all played a big part in bringing the project to a conclusion.

A picture, they tell us, says more than a thousand words, so there must be countless hours of musing in this book for Villa fans. We trust they will enjoy the journey through the first 141 years of one of English football's most famous institutions.....

Early Pride

Aston Villa Football Club, Limited.

Dr. INCOME ACCOUNT, from 30th April, 1896, to 30th April, 1897. Cr.

Dr.	£	s.	d.	£	s.	d.
Wages, Transfers, and Commission paid to and for Players				3,999	10	7
Players' Bonuses for Wins				621	7	6
Match Expenses, viz. :						
[illegible]ravelling, Training, and [illegible]	1,215	4	[illegible]			
Footballs, Jerseys, Boots, and Sundries	79	18	3			
Trainer's Wages and Expenses	153	19	4			
Gatekeepers and Groundmen	218	2	4			
Police	78	13	0			
Referees and Linesmen	80	4	11			
Doctors' Fees, &c.	44	4	6			
				1,870	7	3
Gate Money paid away				1,659	9	9
Printing and Advertising, viz. :						
Stationery, Posters, Tickets, &c. ...	98	2	0			
Posting and Advertising	121	5	10			
				219	7	10
General Expenses, viz :						
Rent, Rates, and Taxes of Ground ...	472	15	11½			
Ground Maintenance and Improvements, &c.	65	2	0½			
Postages and Telegrams	41	18	6			
Association and League Fees	10	0	6			
Petty Payments and Sundries	83	4	9			
Medals for Players	5	16	6			
Club House and Office Rent, Rates, Taxes, Insurance, Gas, Coal, Care-						

Cr.	£	s.	d.
By Members' Subscriptions	268	16	6
,, Season Tickets	191	2	0
,, Gate Money	10,001	8	7
,, Rents	349	5	3
,, Interest on Birmingham Corporation Stock	7	14	8
,, Profit on Sale of Birmingham Corporation Stock	45	12	1
,, Accidental Insurance Compensation (less Premiums paid)	82	0	0
,, Sundry Receipts	40	3	0½

An illuminating look at the balance sheet from well over 100 years ago - in the days when total payments to and for players in a year was well below what even an average Premiership player might expect to receive in a week now.

Grainy images of FA Cup combat over 100 years ago. The setting is White Hart Lane for an FA Cup second-round tie between Tottenham and Villa on February 20, 1904. The visitors led 1-0 at half-time, only for the referee to abandon the game because of an invasion by the packed crowd. A replay was ordered at Villa Park, where Spurs - fined £350 following the trouble in North London - won 1-0.

Villa defend in numbers against an Albion free-kick in a First Division home game on September 21, 1912. The crowd of 55,064 was the biggest Albion had played in front of in the League at that time - and they responded with a 4-2 win set up by a Bob Pailor hat-trick.

Aston Villa 1924-25 style. The club had produced three successive top-six finishes in the First Division but had lost 2-0 in the previous season's FA Cup final to Newcastle - only the second to be staged at Wembley. Pictured are (from left): Blackburn, Miles (trainer), Smart, Moss, Jackson, Milne, Johnston, Ramsay (secretary), Stephenson. Front: York, Kirton, Capewell, Walker, Dorrell, Mort.

Villa's defenders find themselves coming under pressure from the legendary late Everton striker Dixie Dean in a 1920s meeting of the two clubs at Goodison Park in the days when players' shirts did not carry numbers. It was a decade Villa launched by winning the FA Cup and which saw them finishing almost constantly in the upper half of the top flight.

Around World War Two

Berlin, 1938 and Villa take on a German national side including nine Austrian internationals in a May friendly. Villa boss Jimmy Hogan had previously managed Austria and saw his club run out 3-2 winners thanks to two goals from Frank Broome and one from Frank Shell. The three-game tour, containing two wins and a defeat, was marred by controversy over whether Villa players should give the Nazi salute.

Penalty-area congestion in Villa's controversial FA Cup third-round tie against Ipswich in January, 1939. The teams drew 1-1 in the first game but not before Ipswich accused Ernie 'Mush' Callaghan of throwing a lump of mud at the ball a split second before Charlie Fletcher took - and missed - a penalty. In this Portman Road replay, home wing-half Dave Bell broke his leg and Villa won 2-1 thanks to a brace from Fred Haycock. Villa had reached the previous season's semi-final.

The chase is on as Frank Broome, one of the few players to serve Villa before, during and after the war, cuts in towards goal during the 1-1 home draw against Middlesbrough on the last day of the 1938-39 season. Broome, a forward capped seven times by England, netted 16 times in 33 League games in the last full campaign before the hostilities commenced. Villa finished 12th.

Below: The dark shadow of world war was stretching across Britain when Derby's Jack Nicholas scored from this penalty in a League game against Villa at the Baseball Ground on September 2, 1939. It was the last game Villa played before the declaration of hostilities a few days later. By coincidence, the club's first League win back in peace-time also came at Derby, seven long years on.

THE PENALTY OF WAR—FOOTBALL'S LAST FLING

The final whistle has blown, but the crowd at the Baseball Ground on Saturday will long remember this moment whe... ms' captain, Jack Nicholas, sco... match-winning goal with a pena...

DERBY AM...

Villa won the League War Cup North final in 1943-44 and were later beaten Midland Cup finalists after their home had been closed for several wartime seasons for military reasons. With public morale high, though, there were big crowds aplenty when normal competition resumed, with players eager to make up for lost time.

Villa Park was rocking to the beat of 76,500 fans - still a record attendance for any game at the famous old stadium - when Derby won 4-3 in a thrilling FA Cup quarter-final in March, 1946. Here, Peter Doherty forces in to make it 3-3 before Sammy Crooks netted a last-minute decider. Ties that season were played over two legs, with Derby, fourth-round conquerors of Albion, going on to beat Charlton in the final.

Portsmouth keeper Butler looks on anxiously from a prone position as a chance narrowly eludes Trevor Ford during a League game at Villa Park in 1948. Pompey visited the stadium twice in that year, losing 2-1 in the March to goals by Brown and Edwards, then escaping with a 1-1 draw seven months later, when Villa's goal came from Mulraney.

Villa's Con Martin keeps cool to score from a penalty in Ireland's memorable 2-0 victory over England at Goodison Park in September, 1949. England had never lost at that point at home to a nation from overseas while utility man Martin, who was to total 36 caps with the Republic and Northern Ireland, never had a reputation for goals. He netted only once for Villa - from a penalty at Charlton in 1950.

Into the Fifties

Villa press but to little effect during their 2-1 First Division defeat at home to Middlesbrough on November 4, 1950. It was the club's fourth successive game without a victory and they were to trail in a disappointing 15th in the table, also losing 2-1 at Ayresome Park later in the season. Colin Gibson is the player in the middle with the shock of blond hair. The attendance was 37,500.

Another 1950 shot - this time of a happier occasion on November 18 - as Chelsea were sent packing from Villa Park on the receiving end of a 4-2 defeat. Harry Parkes, who was selected in ten different positions in a terrific career of 345 Villa games, is the player about to latch on to this loose ball on a day when the goals came from Johnny Dixon (2), Miller Craddock and Tommy Thompson.

Action from Aston Villa's 2-1 win at Everton on April 21, 1951. Tommy Thompson is the claret and blue predator and Peter Farrell the defender trying to halt his progress. It was the final match of the season at Goodison Park and Villa's success helped ensure the Merseysiders were relegated to the Second Division for the first time in more than 20 years.

Dicky Dorsett tracks back to put in a saving tackle on Albion's right winger Frank Griffin in Villa's victorious short trip to The Hawthorns on December 1, 1951. The club completed the First Division double when the Baggies were beaten 2-0 across the 'patch' in the April. The war years and both clubs' spells out of the top flight had helped see to it that Villa hadn't picked up full points at the venue since April Fool's Day, 1936.

Above: It's 4-1 in this picture in favour of visitors Chelsea but that didn't prevent a header from Colin Gibson flying into the net for the first goal in Villa's 7-1 crushing of the Londoners on April 17, 1952. Gibson netted another later and Billy Goffin helped himself to a hat-trick only three days after the sides had drawn at Stamford Bridge. Villa were destined to finish the season in sixth place.

Villa adopted a dubious look in this third-round FA Cup tie at home to Middlesbrough in January, 1953 - they wore borrowed Birmingham shirts because of a colour clash! Nevertheless, goals from Johnny Dixon, Tommy Thompson and Colin Gibson saw them to a 3-1 victory - only the second time since the war they had won a third-round tie at the first time of asking. Harry Parkes is the Villa man on the ball here.

Derek Pace and Colin Gibson, the latter not to be confused with the defender of the same name from several decades later, acclaim a Villa goal in their clash with Charlton on a mudbath of a pitch at The Valley in the 1950s. But the referee, visible between two lighter-shirted players, is already blowing for an infringement.

Above: Dave Hickson demonstrates the finishing power that Villa missed out on as he shoots the winner on Everton's 1953 FA Cup trip to the Second City. The forward was to join Villa two and a half years later for £17,500 but managed only one goal in 12 games in between two Goodison Park stints that brought him a terrific total of 111 goals in 243 matches.

Danny Blanchflower in characteristic poise in an Aston Villa career of 155 senior games in some three and a half years. Blanchflower, signed from Barnsley in March, 1951, was transferred to Tottenham for £30,000 in 1954-55 and helped make the Londoners the first club to win the League and FA Cup double since Villa in 1897. He was Footballer of the Year twice and played 50 times for Northern Ireland.

Vic Crowe moves across to challenge Cardiff's Ron Stockin during Villa's 2-0 win on August 27, 1955 - their first victory of the season. Crowe, a midfielder born in Wales but raised in Handsworth, went on to play more than 350 games for the club and also picked up 16 senior caps for the Welsh. After a spell with Peterborough, he returned to the Second City and later became manager at Villa Park.

Stan Lynn's reputation as a defender with a venomous shot travelled far and wide - and Albion keeper Jim Sanders was perhaps wise to get nowhere near this decisive penalty! Villa won this game 3-0 on March 16, 1955 to continue their home dominance over the Baggies. Out of eight League meetings of the clubs in the Second City from 1950, they won six and drew two.

Derek Pace slides home the second of his three goals in a 3-2 victory at home to Sheffield United in April, 1956. The Blades were managed at the time by Joe Mercer and were on their way to relegation. Mercer took Pace to Bramall Lane on Boxing Day, 1957 after the Bloxwich-born forward had scored 42 goals in 107 Villa games. And the manager pitched up as boss at Villa Park a year later.

Johnny Dixon demonstrates the instincts that led to him becoming Villa's top scorer for three seasons running in the early 1950s. The brilliant forward, who could play in a variety of positions and later occupied a deeper role, worries Tommy Docherty in the 2-0 home win against Preston on March 30, 1957 - the last leg of a 13-game unbeaten run in League and Cup. Dixon made 430 senior Villa appearances and scored 144 goals.

Billy Walker was an institution at Aston Villa thanks to his 244 goals in 531 League and FA Cup appearances - a scoring record that still stands today. But the long-time skipper, who lit up Villa Park from 1920 to 1933, was no one-club wonder. He later served Nottingham Forest as manager for more than two decades and is seen here celebrating his 21st anniversary at the City Ground with England cricketer Reg Simpson (left) and Forest vice-chairman Jim Wilmour in March, 1960.

Eric Houghton, one of the legends of Villa Park. The pacy winger, capped seven times by England, scored 170 goals in 392 League and FA Cup games for the club and then managed them from 1951 until 1957 after serving Notts County in a similar capacity. With a 1970s stint on the board thrown in just for good measure, he was closely associated with Villa for almost half a century before he died in 1996.

Above: Airborne Johnny Dixon sees his header bounce to safety off no 2 Don Howe in the FA Cup semi-final against Albion at Molineux in 1956-57. On a day when Birmingham were facing Manchester United in the other last-four tie, Villa were often on the receiving end. But two headed goals by no 11 Peter McParland, the second of them five minutes from the end, earned them a 2-2 draw and a replay.
Below: The frantic all-West Midlands battle for a Wembley place moves action moves on to St Andrew's, where Villa held sway - just! That man McParland is close to another goal as he beats the outstretched leg of Don Howe to worry keeper Jim Sanders. It was a game played before 58,067 enthralled fans on what became known as 'Blind-eye Thursday' as it took place on a work-day afternoon in late March when local bosses were resigned to being without tens of thousands of workers. The only goal came from a Billy Myerscough header in the 38th minute and was enough to put Villa in the final for the first time since 1924.

FA Cup Glory

One of the key moments in the 1957 FA Cup final as Manchester United keeper Ray Wood (left) and Villa winger Peter McParland are sprawled out on the turf following a sickening sixth minute collision. Irish international McParland was not punished and was able to continue but Wood was not as lucky, going off with a fractured cheekbone, although he returned shortly before half-time to line up as a winger for nuisance value at a time when substitutes were not permitted.

A happier tale for the other goalkeeper on view at Wembley....Villa's Nigel Sims rushes out to save at the feet of Tommy Taylor, with Pat Saward (left) covering. Taylor perished in the Munish disaster some nine months later.

Peter McParland recovered from the turmoil of his controversial clash with Wood to perform brilliantly. He scored both Villa goals, beating stand-in keeper Jackie Blanchflower in the 65th and 71st minutes, on the second occasion after Dixon had hit the woodwork, and might have had a hat-trick with this cross-shot that flashed narrowly off target. Villa's victory was all the more notable as it had taken Real Madrid to end United's interest in the European Cup at the quarter-final stage only nine days earlier.

Tommy Taylor sets up an anxious final seven minutes for Villa as he pulls a goal back with a looping header from Duncan Edwards' corner. United gambled by restoring Wood to his normal position and playing Blanchflower outfield again in the late onslaught. But the underdogs, superbly led by skipper Johnny Dixon, held on and so succeeded in denying their opponents the honour of pulling off English football's first League and Cup double since Villa had accomplished the feat 60 years earlier.

Reading all about it.....news travels fast when your team are the FA Cup winners!

The joyous homecoming…..Villa's players take the plaudits of the masses back in Birmingham as their coach pulls away from Snow Hill Station. Captain Dixon, a magnificent servant to the club, is the one with the honour of showing off the Cup. Villa's success made them the first club to win the competition seven times. The accompanying front cover of a commemorative menu card shows that players and officials lorded it for the evening when marking their triumph with a bash in the city six days after Wembley.

Chequered Times

Nigel Sims, frustrated at not being able to dislodge the great Bert Williams from the senior goalkeeping jersey at Wolves, crossed the West Midlands in 1956 and proceeded to play 309 Villa first-team games in eight years. Sims, seen here in a 4-3 victory over Newcastle on October 19, 1957, won FA Cup, League Cup and Second Division Championship honours at Villa Park.

Below: Sims goes down to gather safely from Manchester City's Billy McAdams as Vic Crowe keeps a careful watch in the League game between the two clubs at Villa Park on December 14, 1957. Sims and Crowe both served Peterborough in the mid-1960s, in the keeper's case around the time of his two-year stint in Canada. Villa lost this game 2-1 and finished 14th.

August sunshine and a packed Villa Park provide the backdrop to the Second City derby on the opening day of the 1958-59 campaign. Trouble looms here for Villa, though, as a shot by Eddy Brown beats the sprawling Nigel Sims, only for Stan Lynn to clear from near the line. This game was drawn 1-1 and the home side followed up by beating Portsmouth two days later before the rot set in.

New Villa signing Gordon Lee (right) watches Pat Saward clear the danger in Villa's 3-2 defeat at home to Nottingham Forest on September 6, 1958. It was a third successive loss for the side, who crashed 7-2 at West Ham and 5-2 to Portsmouth in their previous two matches.

The dashing Gerry Hitchens is robbed inside the penalty area in Villa's home game against Newcastle on October 4, 1958. The man doing the dispossessing with a well-timed tackle is Bob Stokoe, who later achieved fame as manager of the Sunderland team who beat Leeds in the 1973 FA Cup final. Villa won 2-1, having also prevailed in a five-goal thriller at Blackburn in their previous fixture.

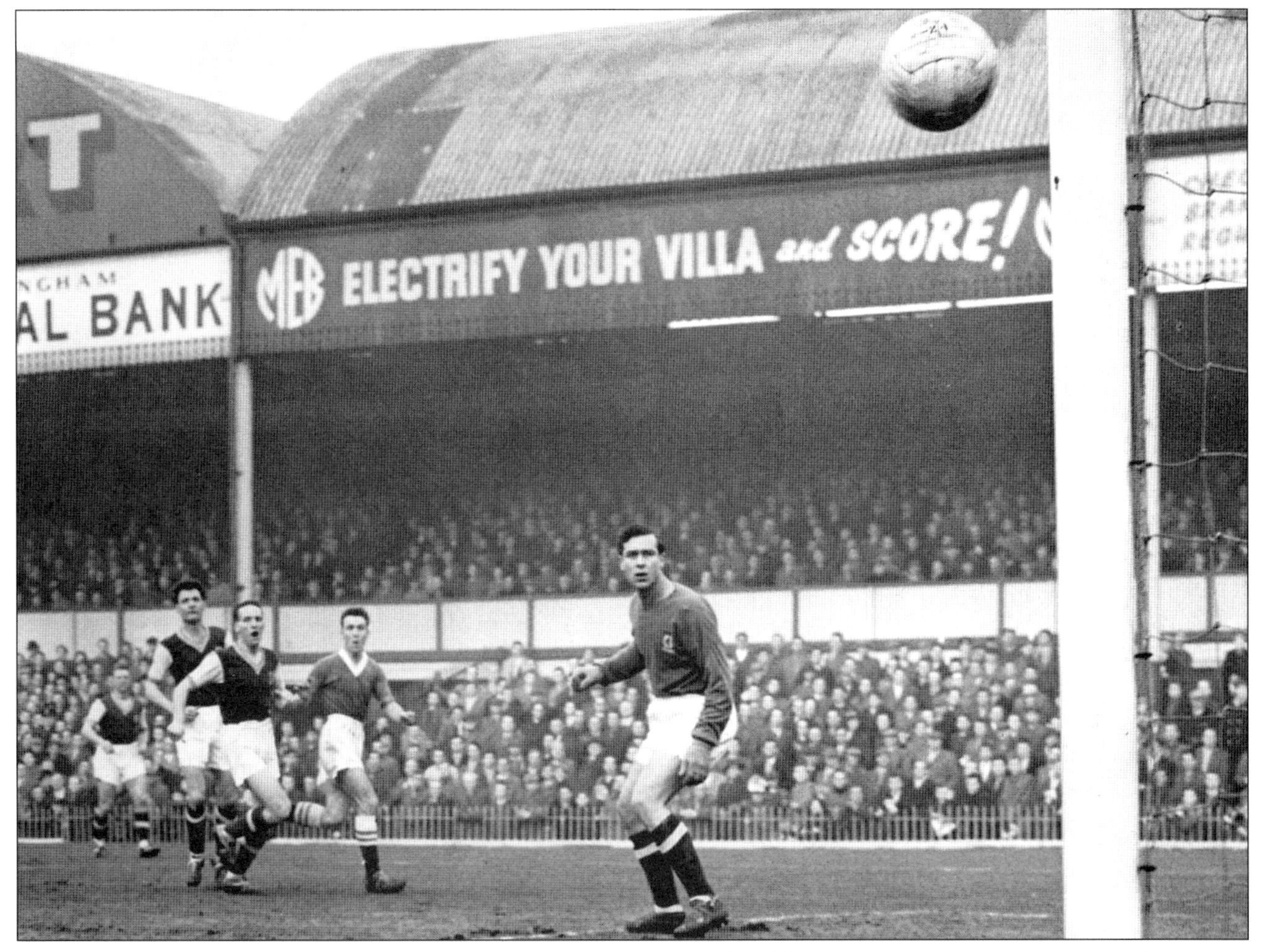

Despairing looks from Villa's defenders and keeper Nigel Sims as an outnumbered Jimmy Greaves puts Chelsea ahead on their visit to Villa Park on January 31, 1959. The lead didn't last long, though, the home side coming back to win 3-1 and so end a damaging sequence of four successive Division One defeats. Alas, the victory did not do much to lift the threat of relegation.

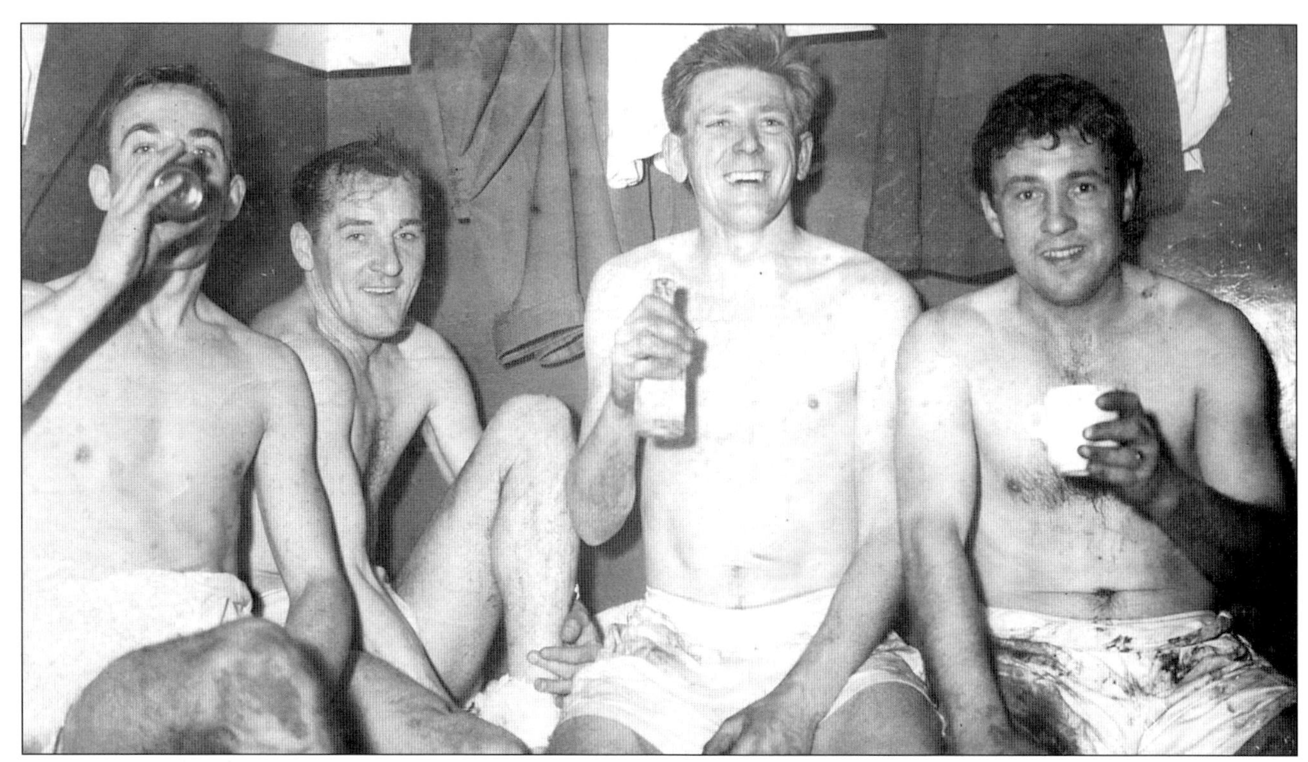

We're in the semis! From left, Ron Wylie, Jackie Sewell, Gerry Hitchens and Leslie Smith celebrate with a drink before washing the mud from their bodies following the FA Cup quarter-final replay at Burnley on March 3, 1959. Villa, held to a goalless home draw a few days earlier, won 2-0 at Turf Moor, where they had lost 3-1 in the League earlier in the season.

A powerful headed clearance by Jimmy Dugdale keeps Luton's attackers at bay as Villa record a third successive League victory in their battle to avoid the drop in March, 1959. Goals by Gerry Hitchens (2) and Leslie Smith saw Villa to a 3-1 win but it wasn't long before the tide turned against them again.

Villa are denied (above) by an unusual save as Charlie 'Chic' Thomson receives a mouthful of ball in the FA Cup semi-final against Nottingham Forest at Hillsborough on March 14, 1959. Villa, who had beaten Rotherham, Chelsea, Everton and Burnley en route, were appearing in a record 16th semi-final but lost 1-0. Below: Ron Wylie is penalised in a tie settled by John Quigley's goal. It gave Forest their first semi-final victory for 61 long years and Billy Walker's side went on to beat Luton in the final.

The falling Ron Wylie sees his header beat keeper Dave McLaren but cleared off the line by left-back Joe Baillie in Villa's clash with Leicester on April 4, 1959. A goal by Johnny Dixon was not enough to save the home side from a 2-1 defeat and they were relegated a few weeks later for the first time since the war after finishing 21st in the table. Portsmouth went down with them while Manchester City escaped by one point and one place.

Five Scots together.....trialists Eric Brodie (left) and Ronnie McIntosh (right) join coach Bill Baxter and dressing-room colleagues Jimmy Goldie and Jackie Hinchcliffe in this all-tartan quintet in the late 1950s. Baxter was a wing-half who played 108 first-team games for the club before moving into the backroom. He is the late father of the current South Africa coach, Stuart Baxter.

Villa come under threat in their 3-1 Second Division home win over Ipswich on September 12, 1959. The team, represented by Jimmy Dugdale in this aerial combat, were in a run of five successive League wins at the time, taking maximum points from this clash with two goals by Peter McParland and one by Ron Wylie. It was form that would sweep them to the Second Division title the following spring.

Jimmy Dugdale gives chase to Birmingham's Eddy Brown in Villa's 2-0 home League defeat in December, 1959. But the side, who had won 5-2 at Sheffield Wednesday in their previous away game, bounced back from this derby-day disappointment by reeling off three straight League victories.

No. 2,874 Price 3d. EVENING DESPATCH Birmingham, Saturday, November 14, 1959

Walsall ten's Cup win : Coventry replay : Blues man ordered off (P.8) and...

VILLA 11, HITCHENS 5

What Price this Villa attack now!

Aston Villa 11, Charlton 1

GERRY HITCHENS slammed his critics today in the best possible way—with five golden goals in this deep humiliation of Charlton.

I don't know what Joe Mercer had to say to his men this week over the recent scarcity of goals. I do know he has been worried about this — and Gerry has been on the verge of being dropped.

Justification for Hitchens, and for Mercer's "unchanged" policy, flowed from this runaway win. There's no room for Ken Price in this forward line at the moment.

Charlton lost goalkeeper Willy Duff in the 60th minute, but Villa were 6—1 by then and the thrashing was well under way.

VILLA WERE RUTHLESS

By then Hitchens had done the damage with his nap-hand.

Villa were ruthless. They were ahead in the second minute, surrendered that lead in th 22nd, but thereafter they went surging forward, slicing open the Charlton defence and ripping it to bits like so much confetti.

VILLA WERE FAST, DIRECT AND FULL OF RUN.

I liked best the way the ball came freely from defence and the way the whole of the forward line moved briskly forward, finding the open spaces. As for their finishing, the score line answers that.

These were Hitchens' first goals for a month and Bobby Thomson weighed in with a couple, his first since mid-September.

Ron Wylie managed one, too, but the clever Scotsman's value stood out greatly as the mid-field schemer with forward passes that would have split any defence in the land.

But for one shaky moment when Charlton scored, Villa's defence was tops and that's fair going against a Charlton forward line that has plenty to offer.

A GREAT SHOW FROM VILLA—THEIR BEST WIN FOR YEARS.

Tightness of defence, quickness on the ball and a forward line in this sort of mood must give them a chance both at the top of the Second Division table, and when the F.A. Cup comes along.

GOAL CHART—Aston Villa: Hitchens (2 mins., 29, 40, 46, 60), Thomson (28, 65), Wylie (63), MacEwan (69), McPar-

★ *It's goal No. 1 coming up* ★

This was the start of the move that brought Villa's two-minute goal at Villa Park. As the Charlton keeper comes out and Bobby Thomson challenges, the scorer, Gerry Hitchens (second from left), moves in to seize his opportunity.

SWINDON'S STORM NOT STRONG ENOUGH . . .

VERDICT by Peter Hewitt

Swindon Town 2, Walsall 3

BE proud of Walsall tonight. They were down to ten men when Peter Billingham limped off after 55 minutes, but a great-hearted defence held out against an almost constant Swindon storm.

Surprise draw for Coventry

COVENTRY 1, SOUTHAMPTON 1

ALTHOUGH Coventry lost 5—1 to Southampton in the League three weeks ago, the Bantams, who have a dismal Cup record, did better than their supporters expected this afternoon.

Skipper Reg Ryan was a great general in the mud of Highfield Road and Ray Straw ...

GOAL CHART—Cov...

A GREAT TWO-GOAL RALLY FAILS TO SAVE ALBION

VERDICT by Alan Lake

Blackburn 3, W.B. Albion 2

ALBION are still hunting their first away victory. The men from The Hawthorns went down 3—2 at Blackburn, after a ten-minute spell of scoring which produced four goals.

Rovers first effort was a fluke goal, Ally MacLeod's shot being deflected by Maurice Setters, but there can be few grumbles about that score.

Albion's defence frequently looked shaky, and Don Howe will have to do better than this when he faces Peter McParland in the international on Wednesday.

The England right back never curbed the lively MacLeod, while Joe Kennedy, too, looked ill at ease against David Whelan, the left-back having his first outing at centre forward.

ROBSON 'THE BEST FORWARD'

Bobby Robson was frequently Albion's "best forward." Though they twice pulled back after being a goal down, this front line is not good enough.

Alec Jackson and Andy Aitken were rarely in the picture, and for long spells Derek Kevan was ploughing a lone path up front.

Skipper Maurice Setters had a quiet match and was never quite able to check Michael England, Blackburn's talented 17-year-old inside left.

GOAL-CHART — Blackburn: MacLeod (40min.); Dobing (68min.); Whelan (77min.). **Albion:** Burnside (70min.); Whitehouse (74min.).

OFFICIAL ATTENDANCE: 18,400.

DAVY BURNSIDE . . . . reduced Albion's arrears.

Then after 68 minutes DOBING made the score 2—0 with a wonder goal.

Two minutes later Burnside scored for Albion.

The game had suddenly burst into life, and in the 74th minute WHITEHOUSE equalised for Albion with a splendid header.

Southern League

Worcester v Yeovil

The Sports Argus cutting of the afternoon some 46 seasons ago when Villa emerged from a goal drought by slamming hapless Charlton 11-1. Gerry Hitchens, whose place in Joe Mercer's attack had been under threat, scored five.

Wolves are out of luck here in the FA Cup semi-final clash with Villa at a packed Hawthorns in April, 1960 - but they had the last laugh. Peter Broadbent, later to play for Villa, is beaten in the air by former Molineux team-mate Nigel Sims, with Jimmy Dugdale (left) and Vic Crowe also pictured in a game in which Wednesbury-born Norman Deeley scored the only goal.

Villa pepper Everton's penalty area during a goal-laden first few weeks back in the top flight. Having started 1960-61 with a 3-2 home win over Chelsea, they lost 5-2 and 5-3 at West Ham and Blackpool respectively before bouncing back to beat the Hammers 2-1 and then post this 3-2 victory, secured by efforts from Gerry Hitchens (2) and Bobby Thomson.

Six months on, Villa returned to the scene of their semi-final heartbreak and found it a much happier occasion. With Gerry Hitchens on the prowl here, they beat Albion 2-0 in front of a Hawthorns crowd of 41,903 and were very much in the derby mood at the time. They had hammered Birmingham 6-2 the previous week.

Harry Burrows, a left-winger who made his name at Villa before underlining his potential in a long spell with Stoke, gives defender Neale a hard time in the 2-0 home victory over Newcastle on October 8, 1960. Villa had lost their two previous games but returned to form thanks to goals by Vic Crowe and Ron Wylie and went on to beat Birmingham 6-2 in their next match.

Two famous Villa Park figures.....Ernie Callaghan and Bob Iverson. Kent-born Iverson was a wing-half or inside-forward who played before, during and after the war for Villa, making 326 appearances for them and becoming a firm favourite with the supporters.

Derek Dougan at the Villa, with and without hair! Right: He tries the famous no 9 shirt for size after his signing from Blackburn in July, 1961. Below: By now shaven-headed, he celebrates Villa's third goal in their victory over Chelsea on August 26, 1961 - a League game played in between the two legs of his new club's League Cup final assignment against Second Division Rotherham. Villa won 3-1 and were destined to enjoy a more than satisfactory campaign on various fronts.

A First League Cup

Anxious looks from goalkeeper Nigel Sims and his defenders as Villa come under pressure in the away first leg of their 1960-61 League Cup final against Rotherham. Alan Kirkman is the forward going close with this diving header and the Yorkshire club, although then in the Second Division, proved troublesome enough to emerge from the Millmoor clash with a 2-0 lead.

Job done! Skipper Vic Crowe shows off the spoils of a thrilling comeback at Villa Park in September, 1961, when Joe Mercer's side clawed back a worrying first-leg deficit to lift the League Cup 3-2 overall. It was the first time a competition that has brought Villa so much success had been staged, its final being held over from the previous season due to fixture congestion. Harry Burrows, Alan O'Neill and Peter McParland scored in front of 30,765 after it stayed goalless on the night until the 67th minute. The rush of goals, the last of them in extra-time, came after Villa had beaten Burnley at Old Trafford in a replayed semi-final.

Joyous scenes in the home dressing room at Villa Park as Aston Villa and the Football League Cup embark on a love affair that has lasted for decades. Skipper Vic Crowe is the man with his hands on the silverware above while, below, defender Jimmy Dugdale, having won the FA Cup with Albion in 1954, is eager for a close-up look at the new trophy.

Start of the Slump

Above: Defender Terry Morrall and keeper Nigel Sims look back in vain as Bobby Smith scores and helps condemn Villa to defeat at White Hart Lane on September 24, 1961. Tottenham were in the latter stages of a run of 11 consecutive wins from the start of a season, so beating the nine victories Hull had reeled off in launching the 1948-49 Third Division North campaign. The crowd at Spurs was 61,356.

Ernie 'Mush' Callaghan (left), one of the true Villa Park greats, is pictured with Sam Keith at the stadium, at the age of 54 in January, 1962. As well as playing in around 300 games for the club from 1930, the full-back or centre-half became their oldest ever player at 39 years 257 days old in April, 1947. He also won the BEM during the war for his 'conspicuous bravery' as a reserve policeman in an air raid.

Derek Dougan takes careful aim and shoots goalwards against his visiting former club Blackburn at the start of February, 1962. The Doog had played in the 1961 League Cup final success over Rotherham and was to score 26 goals in his 60-game first team career in the Second City before he was off again onhis varied travels. Villa beat Rovers 1-0 and so recorded their first victory in seven League matches.

Villa were bystanders on a red-letter Suffolk day when unable to prevent Alf Ramsey's Ipswich winning 2-0 in the spring of 1962 and so lift the League Championship for the first time in their history. At a packed Portman Road, the ball is destined here for the far post, where Ray Crawford appears to have sneaked goal-side of John Sleeuwenhoek. Ipswich also ended Villa's reign as League Cup holders that season.

Villa's sun-tanned players are welcomed back to their Trinity Road training ground by Joe Mercer following the 1962 summer break. The club had finished seventh the previous season but were to find the going tougher next time round.

Jimmy McEwan slips the ball under the body of diving Blackpool keeper Tony Waiters to put his side in front in a First Division game at Villa Park on September 1, 1962. The Seasiders, also represented in this picture by right-back and England World Cup man Jimmy Armfield, now a BBC radio summariser, hit back to draw 1-1 and confirm a downturn for Joe Mercer's men after they had started the season with three wins and then a defeat.

With keeper Roy Bailey grounded and Ron Wylie looking on, Derek Dougan swings his left foot but is unable to force the ball home in the 4-2 victory over Ipswich in late September, 1962. The game completed a highly eventful week for the centre-forward, who had been sent off against Nottingham Forest the week before, then scored a League Cup hat-trick against his former club Peterborough and was finally named in the Northern Ireland squad for the visit to Poland.

One of the most star-studded line-ups in Villa Park history. Sadly, they weren't representing the club! This gifted collection were merely playing (and losing) a practice match against Villa prior to turning out for the Football League against the Italian League at Highbury in November, 1962. Back row (from left): Gordon Banks, George Eastham, Brian Miller, Jimmy Greaves, John Connelly, Les Allen, Mike O'Grady, Bryan Douglas. Front row: Bobby Moore, Jimmy Armfield, Ron Springett, Ron Flowers, Brian Labone, Ray Wilson. Fittingly, this get-together came in the month Villa Park was named as one of the venues for the 1966 World Cup.

Right: Keeper Geoff Sidebottom repels this Blues attack in the Second City derby on March 16, 1963. John Sleeuwenhoek and Jimmy Harris are the other players closing in on the ball. Villa won 4-0 with goals by Phil Woosnam, Alan Baker, Alan Deakin and Harry Burrows (pen), but Blues won that spring's two-leg League Cup final between the clubs.

Below: Don Megson, father of the latter-day Albion manager, foils Derek Dougan as Villa press at home to Sheffield Wednesday on April 13, 1963. Villa lost 2-0 - their sixth straight defeat in a run that stretched to an horrific club record 11 after they stood fifth in December. Dougan moved in the summer of 1963 to Peterborough, the fee of £21,000 netting the club a £6,000 profit.

Ground improvement work continued at Villa Park as preparations started for the 1966 World Cup finals in England. Part of the upgrade was a new roof for the Witton Lane Stand. The alterations, carried out in 1963, cost £40,000 but the club were given a loan of £9,900 in recognition of being one of the chosen venues for the world's biggest football tournament and were reimbursed to the tune of £46,000.

Where did that one go? Puzzled looks and wayward glances abound as a Villa attack led by Tony Hateley (right) peters out in the Blackburn Rovers penalty area during the League clash of the two clubs on the last day of August, 1963. The Blackburn player in the foreground is centre-half Mike England, who scored an own goal to give Villa hope in their 2-1 defeat.

All action in the Albion goalmouth as Villa press from a corner in the Hawthorns derby clash on October 12, 1963. From left, Phil Woosnam, John Sleeuwenhoek, Tony Hateley and Jimmy McEwan are the players putting the Baggies under pressure on a day Villa scored through Hateley, Mike Tindall and a Ray Crawford own goal - but still contrived to lose 4-3!

Over the bar goes this header from Tony Hateley during the visit of Ipswich on November 29, 1963. Villa could have done with it going in as they were held to a disappointing 0-0 draw by a side rooted to the foot of the table and destined for relegation. Hateley had scored twice in the previous home game - a 4-0 win over Manchester United - to take his season's League goal tally into double figures.

Don't be confused, it *is* a Villa home game.....a white-shirted Tony Hateley causes trouble for the Aldershot defence in the third-round FA Cup showdown on January 4, 1964. The tie was played in the days when home clubs changed strip in the event of a colour clash in the competition - and it proved to be a real tale of woe for Villa, with this 0-0 draw followed by a 2-1 defeat in the replay against the Fourth Division club at the Recreation Ground.

Left-winger Harry Burrows takes evasive action as Leicester defender King clears his lines in the East Midlanders' 3-1 victory at Villa Park on April 18, 1964. Ron Wylie is in the background, the thinly spaced crowd reflecting Villa's struggles at the time. Joe Mercer had stood down as manager, partly because of ill health, and it was left to his assistant Dick Taylor to steer the club to safety a precarious two places outside the relegation zone.

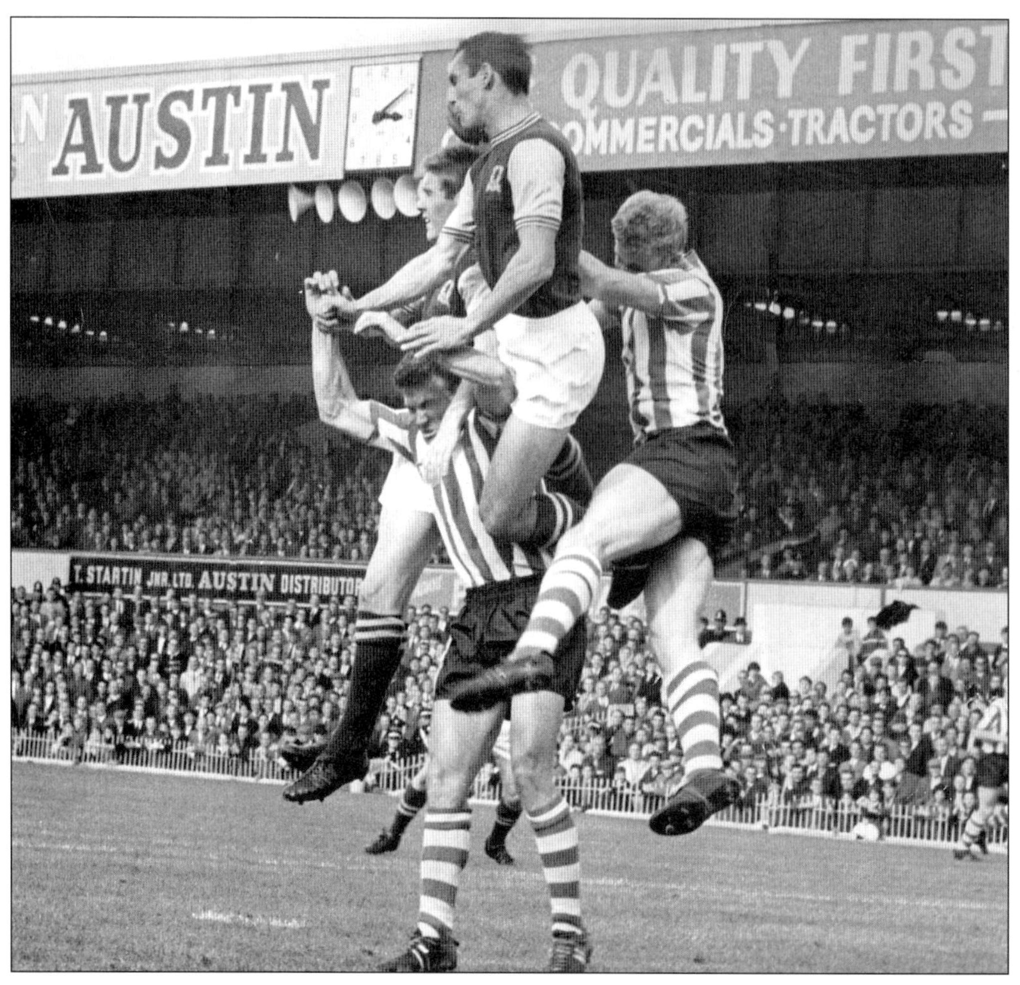

Left: New season, same problems. Villa were still anything but a potent force in the top flight in 1964-65 as, under the permanent management of Dick Taylor, they limped across the finishing line in 16th place. They were strong at home, though, and coped on September 19 with the challenge of Sheffield Wednesday, whose Gerry Young is grounded in this two v two tussle in which Tony Hateley appears to be coming out on top.

Below: Visiting Albion held the derby aces despite a numerical disadvantage for part of this clash on October 17, 1964. A single goal from Gerry Howshall won it on a day when the Baggies had their skipper Graham Williams sent off for an incident involving Tony Hateley. Here, Geoff Sidebottom takes the ball under threat from John Kaye as Gordon Lee ducks. It was Villa's fourth League defeat in a row.

Bowed heads from Villa players in memory of the great Billy Walker, who had died at the age of 67 a few hours before this game against Burnley at Villa Park on November 28, 1964. Wednesbury-born Walker, a wonderful servant to the club before going on to manage elsewhere, passed away in a Nottingham hospital after a long illness. He won 18 caps for England, several of them as skipper.

Johnny MacLeod, a busy winger who won four senior Scotland caps, gave Arsenal a reminder of his abilities when he touched in this goal in a 3-1 Villa win just before Christmas, 1964. MacLeod had played 112 senior games for the Gunners before joining Villa for £35,000 three months before this game. At Villa Park, he scored 18 times in 139 games before embarking on a spell in Belgium.

Villa became feared League Cup opponents in the 1960s but that didn't prevent them putting near-neighbours Coventry to the sword in the FA Cup on third-round day in 1965. A 3-0 win ensured First Division supremacy, with John Sleeuwenhoek spectacularly clearing this cross above, watched by Ron Wylie, Dave Pountney and Charlie Aitken. At the same time, Villa were on their way to their third League Cup semi-final in five years. Below: Tipton-born Alan Baker congratulates Tony Hateley - later of the Sky Blues - on scoring the side's first goal. The dejected goalkeeper is Bill Glazier.

Phil Woosnam narrowly fails to connect with a Harry Burrows centre as the clock ticks down towards extra-time in Villa's 0-0 FA Cup fifth-round draw at Wolves on February 24, 1965. Fred Davies gathers safely and the Molineux men, having drawn 1-1 at Villa Park, won 3-1 in the second replay at The Hawthorns. The first two games in the trilogy were watched by a total of 100,000 spectators.

No luck for Phil Woosnam on April 17, 1965, as he hits the post in the League visit of a Sheffield United side Villa had beaten at Bramall Lane in that season's FA Cup fourth round. The Midlanders won this clash as well, 2-0, and stood up well to a punishing end-of-season schedule. They finished the campaign with seven games in 18 days and stayed unbeaten throughout them. The keeper here is Alan Hodgkinson.

Taking to the skies....Villa's players and officials climb aboard ready for the short flight to Holland and their two-game summer tour in 1965. The club were involved in two entertaining draws in the Netherlands, 3-3 against Utrecht and then 2-2 against Twente Entschede. It was a special trip for centre-half John Sleeuwenhoek, whose father was a Dutch parachute instructor.

Heading for a Fall

Charlie Aitken was anything but a renowned scorer while compiling his club record 660 Aston Villa appearances - a vast tally that brought him only 16 goals. But he netted one with this fine header, watched by Phil Woosnam, in the 2-2 draw with Leicester on August 29, 1965. Tony Hateley was responsible for Villa's other goals after they had started the season with two defeats.

Trouble looms for Blackpool on September 11, 1965 as that man Phil Woosnam steers home a fine header in a 3-0 home win at Villa Park. Woosnam, a university graduate and 17-cap Welsh international, was signed from West Ham in November, 1962 and scored 30 goals in 125 senior games for the club before embarking on a lucrative career on and off the field in America. Villa made it four victories in a row by winning 6-3 at Fulham the following week.

Tony Hateley's face is about to light up as he watches his header to a left-wing centre disappear into the top of the net for Villa's third goal in their 3-2 victory over Everton on December 12, 1965. The hapless opponents are grounded goalkeeper Geoff Barnett and England centre-half Brian Labone. Villa had also scored three the previous week in a draw at Arsenal.

ELT BROS. LTD.
THE MAIN VAUXHALL DEALERS
Tel. SPR. 3606
SHAFTMOOR LANE, B'HAM 28

Evening Mail and Despatch

Sports Argus

CITY FINAL

First-tim
get a great
at Damson
£16
See you at
off L
Sunday

SATURDAY, MARCH 19, 1966 — The FAMOUS sports paper — No. 31,172 — 4d.

Tottenham lead 5–1 ... leader lashes hat-trick

HATELEY'S 4 SPUR VILLA

Four-goal fight-back for draw

by FRED DONE

Tottenham Hotspur 5 Aston Villa 5

FOUR goals by Hateley featured a tremendous Aston Villa fight-back against Spurs at White Hart Lane today, and the Midlanders fully deserved their 5-5 draw after being 1-5 down.

Spurs were three goals up in 12 minutes. Then Villa rolled up their sleeves. Hateley made it 3-1, and added three further goals in the second half.

Deakin was moved up to inside-left to partner Baker. Pountney filled the wing half vacancy and with MacLeod a victim of laryngitis, MacEwan made his first senior appearance of the season on the right wing.

Spurs relied on the side beaten

● TENSE . . . is the word for the expression of Thwaites (centre) and Vowden, as the inside-left rounds Beech in this Blues attack.

FLASH FOCUS

ALVECHURCH

ALVECHURCH'S ambitious bid to play at Wembley next month in the final of the F.A. Amateur cup was marred by a missed penalty kick at Stamford Bridge today. Wealdstone went in front in the [illegible] minute.

Cocking took the spot kick when Jones was unfairly brought down in the 25th minute, but gave Wealdstone's goalkeeper, Paisley, an easy shot to save.

It was a disappointing goalkeeping mistake by Smith which put the Midlanders behind when he punched a long lob from Allen into his own net.

The tie was a keenly-contested one in which the Midland supporters did not take kindly to some rugged tackling by the Wealdstone defenders. But Alvechurch were continually surprising the Londoners by their good football on a dry pitch which made the ball

Another Villa goal glut! Unfortunately, hosts Tottenham were similarly prolific on this extraordinary day in the spring of 1966, which was particularly memorable for Tony Hateley. He scored four to inspire his side to recover from a horrific opening 12 minutes in which they conceded three after letting in five against Fulham the week before. Spurs later led 5-1 before being sensationally pegged back.

Did they ***really*** play in that?

A brief look back to when football was more inclined to just get on with it...in any weather

It's not shaken camera syndrome - the blur was caused by the rain! Willie Hamilton goes in bravely with his head as Doug Fraser lunges in foot-first in the First Division derby at Albion on December 19, 1965. The game was abandoned at 0-0 just after half-time because of waterlogging and drawn 2-2 when re-staged a few weeks later. Curiously, Villa's match at home to West Ham, straight after the original Albion fixture, was also abandoned.

Charlie Aitken and no 5 John Sleeuwenhoek do battle with Blackburn's Harrison in a goalless top-flight draw at Villa Park on January 19, 1963. Such was the icy snap that this was the only League game Villa played in that month - and their FA Cup third-round tie at Bristol City, drawn 1-1 in January, wasn't replayed until March 7.

Willie Hamilton skates across the icy surface to send a shot through the snowflakes and into the Nottingham Forest net in a resounding home win on January 15, 1966. It was Villa's third goal in a 3-0 victory. Hamilton won senior recognition from Scotland, picked up a League Cup winners' medal north of the border with Hearts and scored nine times in 54 first-team games for Villa.

When Christmases were white.....this was one day when the elements had the last word. A deserted Villa Park provides a wintry outlook over the festive period in the 1961-62 season.

Erdington-born Colin Withers, who tried his luck with both Albion and Birmingham before embarking on an Aston Villa career of 163 appearances between 1964 and 1969, dashes from his line to block well from Liverpool's Roger Hunt in a 3-0 home defeat on March 26, 1966. Hunt was to play a prominent role in England's triumphant World Cup campaign a few months later.

A spectacular aerial shot of Villa Park in all its glory during the 1966 World Cup finals. This picture was taken just after kick-off in the group game between Spain and eventual finalists West Germany. The stadium also staged both Spain's 2-1 defeat against Argentina and the South Americans' goalless draw with the Germans. All three matches were watched by well over 40,000.

Lew Chatterley holds off Keith Kettleborough's challenge to crash home Villa's first goal of the 1966-67 season - a campaign that was to prove the club's last in the top flight for eight years. This strike came on August 20 and was watched by no 9 Tony Hateley but it wasn't enough to bring a victory. Visitors Newcastle headed back to the north east with a 1-1 draw.

Lew Chatterley raises his arms aloft in celebration of opening the scoring in a 3-0 win against visiting Manchester City on October 5, 1966 - a feat that brought a toilet roll unfurling from the Holte End; a common sight in 1960s and 1970s football. City were just promoted to the top flight and were under the management of former Villa boss Joe Mercer.

Typical Tony Hateley.....bursting between Liverpool's Tommy Smith and Ron Yeats to power in a header on October 2, 1966. Hateley, who broke his rib in this 3-2 defeat on the day John Woodward made his debut, scored twice and impressed Bill Shankly, who signed him a year later after a spell at Chelsea. He had top-scored three seasons in a row and netted a tremendous 86 goals in 148 Villa games.

It's the winner for Keith Bradley in the victory at home to Sunderland on December 28, 1966. Bobby Park and Dave Pountney are the team-mates rushing to congratulate him while Jim Baxter is the visiting player on the left in the foreground with his hands on his hips. This was one of only two goals wing-half Bradley scored in 144 senior appearances for Villa - and it came only 24 hours after Villa had lost 2-1 at Sunderland.

Derek Dougan back at Villa - but by now in the colours of Leicester. The striker climbs above John Sleeuwenhoek and Mick Wright in this incident on February 4, 1967 in a game won 1-0 by the visitors. Earlier in the season, Villa lost 5-0 at Filbert Street, with The Doog chipping in with a hat-trick. In a bad time for the club at the feet of former team-mates, they also saw Harry Burrows score three against them for Stoke in December, 1966.

Below: A brave block by keeper Colin Withers denies Liverpool's Ian St John on this occasion during Villa's unrewarding double-header at Anfield in the late winter of 1967. The side lost 1-0 at the ground on February 11 in the on-going battle for top-flight survival and by the same scoreline in the fourth round of the FA Cup a week later, having won at Preston in the third round.

HEADING FOR A FALL

Off to the bracing air of Lytham St Anne's are trainer Bill Baxter and (from left) Barry Stobart, Dave Pountney, John Sleeuwenhoek, Johnny MacLeod and Charlie Aitken. The 1967 seaside trip was planned as a spring tonic in the struggle to avoid relegation. Alas, Villa were promptly beaten 3-1 at Manchester United, 4-2 by Everton and 6-2 at Southampton and went down with, ironically, Blackpool. Not surprisingly, manager Dick Taylor paid for the drop with his job and Baxter was one of those who went with him.

Still Sliding

Willie Anderson, signed from Manchester United in 1967, fires the last goal in a 3-1 home victory over Rotherham that suggested Villa, after two opening defeats, were adapting to Second Division life.

Above: Another game, another goal. Brian Godfrey slides in to beat Birmingham keeper Jim Herriott and mark his first Villa home appearance with a goal on October 8, 1967. The Blues recovered to win 4-2 but lost at the stadium the following April in the FA Cup semi-final against Albion.

A crash landing for Brian Greenhalgh after heading his side's second goal at home to Hull on November 20, 1967. Villa were still sliding, though, and lost 3-2. Greenhalgh had arrived, like Godfrey, from Preston but their new club were to finish a miserable 16th.

Villa had one of the oldest boards in English football in 1967-68, headed by (centre) chairman Norman Smith - a club director since 1939. Also present between (far left) secretary Fred Archer and (far right) new boss Tommy Cummings are George Robinson, vice-chairman Bruce Normansell, Bill Lovsey and Joe Heath. Normansell and Lovsey had been on the board since the mid-1950s and Heath from 1961.

Hang on, who's that defender tracking back? Ron Atkinson cuts a burly figure as he unsuccessfully tries to stave off a Villa attack in the home League game against Oxford on September 29, 1968. Big Ron is too late to prevent Brian Godfrey flashing in his side's second goal in a pressure-easing 2-0 win. The keeper is Jim Barron, who was Atkinson's no 2 on the managerial side at Villa Park in the 1990s.

More action from Villa's victory at home to Oxford in the autumn of 1968, with keeper Jim Barron this time pushing wide a shot from Wearside-born inside-forward Tommy Mitchinson.

Supporter and shareholder strife has been an occasional downside to Villa Park life over the decades. Digbeth Civic Hall was the setting for this fans' protest meeting on November 22, 1968 - 11 days after Tommy Cummings was sacked as manager. The club hadn't won for two months and the board met for a five-hour emergency meeting the previous night. They then resigned en bloc in the December.

Left: Barrie Hole hits Villa's second goal past Southampton keeper Gerry Gurr in the FA Cup fourth-round clash at The Dell in January, 1969. Villa managed a 2-2 draw and won the replay 2-1 against the top-flight club, who had been knocked out in a round-four replay by Albion the year before.

Below: Outside right Dave Rudge celebrates Villa's first goal in their welcome 2-0 victory at home to Portsmouth in February, 1969. The breakthrough followed keeper John Milkins' save from an effort by Willie Anderson.

Back on the FA Cup trail - and Villa put up spirited resistance before slipping to a 3-2 fifth-round defeat against 1967 winners Tottenham on February 12, 1969. All the goals came in the second half of an exciting tie, which featured this Barrie Hole goal that evened things up at 1-1 following the first of Jimmy Greaves' two goals. Peter Broadbent was Villa's other scorer.

Left: Dave Rudge takes aim but misses out with this right-foot shot on a winter wonderland of a Villa Park surface on February 15, 1969. Up in support with him is no 10 Lionel Martin. The opposition are Bury, who became Villa's sixth victims in seven League matches as they were beaten 1-0. Wolverhampton-born Rudge advanced through the ranks at the club and totalled 60 first-team appearances for Villa. Tommy Docherty had breezed in as Villa boss a few weeks earlier following a brief caretaker stint by Arthur Cox - and the club's gates increased substantially, with more than 59,000 watching the Cup replay success over Southampton. The club's fortunes went the same way and the surge towards safety was up and running.

Below: Villa's players, accompanied by chairman Doug Ellis, manager Tommy Docherty and commercial manager Eric Woodward, depart for a tournament in the United States in the summer of 1969. Also competing were Kilmarnock, Dundee United, West Ham and the eventual winners Wolves. In addition, Villa played an exhibition game against Atlanta Chiefs, the club for whom Phil Woosnam had worked after leaving England.

Villa's £100,000 new boy Bruce Rioch - a signing from Luton - gets weighed in by first-team trainer Arthur Cox (left) and youth coach Graham Leggatt before the start of the 1969-70 season. Awaiting their turns at the scales are (from left) Rioch's brother Neil, Pat McMahon and Chico Hamilton. All four players had arrived at the club that summer.

Villa, in radical new kit, made a troubled start to what would have been Tommy Docherty's first full season - if he hadn't been sacked half-way through! For the second time in three years, they were knocked out of the League Cup by Albion, this time 2-1 in round two. Home keeper Evan Williams beats Colin Suggett and John Talbut to this cross after Villa had won at Chester in the previous round.

Busy times for Vic Crowe.... right, as reserve manager, he wishes Brian Little (left) and Roy Stark luck before the two 15-year-olds make their reserve debuts in the Central League game at Manchester United in the autumn of 1969. All Villa fans know what became of Little but Stark's career was less fulfilled. After skippering the club to glory in the 1971-72 FA Youth Cup, he made only two first-team appearances.
Crowe, brought back by Villa after a stint in America with Atlanta Chiefs, found himself upgraded from reserve boss to manager with the sacking of Tommy Docherty. And he was eager to put his mark on the club. But the League position was precarious with the season more than half spent by the time he got to work (below) with his squad. George Curtis, next but one to Crowe towards the middle of the picture, had just been signed from Coventry.

No luck for the grounded Andy Lochhead on his Villa debut at home to Bristol City on February 21, 1970 - and no goals in 12 League games for the club at the end of that season. The ex-Burnley and Leicester striker was recruited for £30,000 from Filbert Street and was to flourish into a bargain buy following his initial struggles to make an impact. Bristol won 2-0 and Villa duly plunged into Division Three for the first time in their history after finishing one place above wooden spoonists Preston and two points behind Charlton.

Off the mark at last......Andy Lochhead rises above defender Stuart Robertson to head his first Villa goal. It came five minutes into the home game against Doncaster on September 5, 1970, and set his side on the way to a 3-2 victory - their third win of the five-game-old League season. The former Scottish under-21 international striker's wait for a breakthrough had stretched 17 long matches.

League Cup Lifeline

Pat McMahon beats former Albion keeper Dick Sheppard to put Villa into the semi-finals of the 1970-71 League Cup. This goal saw off Bristol Rovers in a Villa Park replay on November 25 after Vic Crowe's side had defeated Notts County, Burnley, Northampton and Carlisle in the earlier rounds. The victory came at a time when the club were also pushing hard for promotion from the Third Division.

Andy Lochhead is out of luck with this header at Manchester United in the first leg of the League Cup semi-final on December 16, 1970. He was on target, though, in the first half of a 1-1 draw watched by around 10,000 Villa fans - and even a quick Brian Kidd equaliser failed to douse the delight at a tough job superbly done. The tie had been delayed for a week by power cuts.

The memorable moments that spelled club history on December 23, 1970. Above: It's that man Lochhead again, escaping the attentions of Ian Ure and keeper Alex Stepney to nod Villa's second-half equaliser from a Brian Godfrey free-kick in the League Cup semi-final second leg against star-studded Manchester United. Below: Pat McMahon is the match-winning hero as he turns home the decider after 73 minutes with no 6 David Sadler and centre-half Ure helpless to intervene. Brian Kidd, another survivor from United's European Cup winning side only two years earlier, had opened the scoring on the night. The result meant the most famous club in Britain had been brought down over two epic games by a side playing in the Third Division.

Another view of the dramatic late Pat McMahon goal that brought Third Division Villa the scalp of mighty Manchester United and sent them to Wembley. It was a reminder that Villa remained a huge club, albeit one languishing following a nightmare couple of years. It was an astonishing conquest given that Villa had lost 3-1 in the FA Cup first round at Torquay barely a month earlier.

Have a sip of this - we're off to Wembley! In the joyous setting of the home dressing room, Bruce Rioch finds the drink's on him as Doug Ellis cracks open the Moet. Ian 'Chico' Hamilton watches the high jinks before treating himself to a taste. Keeper John Dunn, partly hidden by the chairman's arm, opts for something a little more down-to-earth - and decides it's lighting-up time. Villa had beaten mighty Manchester United 3-2 on aggregate.

The 1970-71 League Cup final proved a great day out for Villa and their fans despite the 2-0 defeat inflicted on them by hot favourites Tottenham. They had a good go at upsetting the form-book once more but couldn't make the most of this half-chance (above) from which Chico Hamilton worried Pat Jennings, the close-marking Cyril Knowles and England man Martin Peters. There were only 12 minutes left when the deadlock was finally broken by Martin Chivers, who then left the underdogs floored with this killer second (below) through a goalmouth strewn with claret and blue shirts.

The Long Climb Back

Aston Villa v Walsall in a League game? It sounds unlikely but it happened on March 17, 1971, when Harry Gregory found Saddlers' former Albion defender Stan Jones getting a bit too close for comfort to him following a challenge on keeper Bob Wesson. The 0-0 draw ensured the local bragging rights stayed with Walsall, who had beaten their illustrious neighbours 3-0 at the turn of the year.

Villa found Walsall a surprisingly tough nut to crack in the Third Division, drawing three and losing one of four meetings with them. Here, on August 21, 1971, Charlie Aitken (left) and keeper John Dunn are powerless to prevent John Manning scoring in the 1-1 draw at Saddlers' old Fellows Park home in Villa's first away fixture of the season. Vic Crowe's side had already beaten visiting Plymouth.

Willie Anderson, a one-time understudy to George Best at Manchester United, had the incredible record of scoring in five games against Wrexham in 1971-72, including (above) this penalty-kick equaliser in an autumnal League Cup second replay at The Hawthorns. Villa played the Welshmen twice in the Third Division as well as eventually beating them in this three-game epic.

Middle left: Dave Gibson jumps for joy after helping in Neil Rioch's shot for the third goal in Villa's 4-1 Third Division home win against Blackburn Rovers on October 3, 1971. It was the inside-forward's only goal in 24 appearances for the club after joining them on a free transfer from Leicester. He also won seven senior caps for Scotland. The week after this game, Villa drew 4-4 at Port Vale and then sensationally won 6-0 away to Oldham shortly afterwards.

Below left: If proof were needed of Aston Villa's formidable crowd-pulling potential, it came in this famous Third Division clash on February 12, 1972. An astonishing attendance of 48,110, plus the BBC Match of the Day cameras, turned up to witness the 2-1 defeat of promotion rivals Bournemouth - one of 14 Villa victories in a wonderful 16-game spell. Here, Geoff Vowden beats former Wolves goalkeeper Fred Davies to nod in the much-needed equaliser. Three more of Villa's home games that season were to attract 40,000-plus gates.

Above: Entry of the greatest......Pele, the world's finest footballer, comes to Villa Park. An incredible crowd of 54,437 witnessed this friendly against Brazilian giants Santos on February 21, 1972, with Villa winning 2-1 thanks to goals by Ray Graydon (penalty) and Pat McMahon. Because of power cuts, the club had paid for a generator to ensure the Midlands had a glimpse of the star turn of the 1970 World Cup. Villa reserve Mike Hoban, later a successful player and coach in the US, had special reason to remember the big night. He won Pele's shirt afterwards in a raffle organised among the Villa players.

A key signing in the Aston Villa revival. Manager Vic Crowe is all smiles as he unveils his £90,000 new boy, Chris Nicholl, a dominant centre-half recruited from Luton in March, 1972. Although Cheshire-born, Nicholl was to make 51 senior appearances for Northern Ireland and turn out in 252 League and cup games for Villa, including the 1977 League Cup final, in which he scored spectacularly in the replay.

Villa's lads made history late in April, 1972 when beating Liverpool 5-2 on aggregate and winning the FA Youth Cup for the first time in the club's history. Roy Stark is the delighted skipper raising the silverware, flanked by Tony Betts and keeper Jake Findlay. Betts and Brian Little (2) scored in a memorable 4-2 win at Anfield after Scouser John Gidman had scored the only goal of the first leg from a penalty.

Another 1971-72 prize came Villa's way when captain Bruce Rioch received the Third Division champions' trophy from Football League president Len Shipman. Villa topped the table by five points from Brighton in the days of two points for a win. This presentation on a rain-lashed May night was followed by a 1-0 win over Chesterfield - the club Villa had played in their first game in Division Three.

Promoted together, Villa and Brighton didn't have to wait long in 1972-73 to meet again at a higher level. Midfielder Geoff Vowden links up here with Ian Ross, a defender signed from Liverpool for £70,000 in the previous February, in the 1-1 draw between the clubs in the Second Division in early September. Villa had soon clicked into gear with three victories out of four and were to fall just short in the race for promotion for the second successive season.

Having finished third in 1972-73, well behind Burnley and QPR respectively, Villa aimed to go one better the following season. And they made a decent start with this Charlie Aitken goal (one of only 16 the left-back scored in passing Billy Walker's appearance tally for the club) helping them to a 2-0 win over Preston on August 25, 1973 - part of an unbeaten start-of-season run of seven League games.

Bruce Rioch takes aim and scores with this characteristic left-foot drive from more than 20 yards in the home game against Leyton Orient on September 22, 1973. The goal came from a free-kick laid off short by no 10 Geoff Vowden after only 67 seconds. Orient were to just miss out on promotion, condemned to another Second Division year when Villa drew 1-1 at Brisbane Road at the end of the season.

Sammy Morgan celebrates with Geoff Vowden after scoring a tremendous goal in the 1-1 FA Cup draw against Arsenal at Highbury in January, 1974. The Northern Ireland international striker, sent off later in the game after a clash with keeper Bob Wilson, was bought from Port Vale, a year or so after the arrival from Liverpool of Alun Evans (far right) - once Britain's most expensive teenage footballer.

And Morgan was the hero in the Villa Park replay against the Gunners as well. He gets behind Arsenal's defence here and launches himself at a centre to head Villa into a first-half lead in the replay. Alun Evans made the final score 2-0 and Villa had the scalp of the 1971 double winners, only to lose at Burnley in the next round.

Well, he was a fast bowler in a previous life! Albion centre-forward David Shaw looks on with admiration as former Baggies keeper Jim Cumbes prepares to send a huge throw down-field in the Boxing Day derby defeat at The Hawthorns in 1973. In the background is West Brom record-breaker Tony Brown, whose son Paul has worked in the Villa Park media office in recent years.

Bobby Thomson, formerly of Birmingham, Wolves and England, combines with keeper Graham Horn to clear Luton's lines in their League clash at Villa Park in the middle of 1973-74. Sammy Morgan and Ray Graydon are the attackers in view. Luton were to be promoted as runners-up to Middlesbrough while Villa, disappointingly, finished just below half-way.

Sammy Morgan takes sensible evasive action and leaves the way clear for Brian Little to drive a shot past keeper Jimmy Allan and centre-half Ron Potter in Villa's home clash with Swindon on April 8, 1974. The attacker to the left is Keith Leonard. The Wiltshire club were destined to finish bottom of the table while Villa were to trail in 11 places lower than the previous season in 14th.

Bobby Campbell and no 11 Brian Little are shut out by a brave lunge by Jim Montgomery in Villa's home League game against Sunderland on April 21, 1974. While Little went on to achieve great things and also have a successful spell as manager, Campbell moved on early in 1975 and had a long and varied career that stretched to some 600 appearances with Northern Ireland and his many clubs.

Whack! Chico Hamilton connects sweetly with a left-foot shot and scores Villa's sixth and final goal in their annihilation of Hull on August 27, 1974. The Humbersiders could find no reply on a night when Sammy Morgan scored three to announce that the new Ron Saunders era was well and truly up and running. Looking on in is John Robson, previously a League Championship winner with Derby.

A League Cup glory night for Villa early in a run that was to end in triumph at Wembley. Having drawn 1-1 at home to Everton, Second Division Villa produced one of the shocks of the season on September 19, 1974 to take Goodison by storm and run out handsome 3-0 winners. Here, Ray Graydon scores a beauty with Roger Kenyon and keeper David Lawson powerless to intervene.

After Goodison, there was an earthier feel to Villa's next League Cup assignment, at Fourth Division Crewe. And they were happy to emerge with a 2-2 draw. From left, Sammy Morgan, Keith Leonard and Chico Hamilton celebrate after Morgan had beaten former Villa keeper Geoff Crudgington to make it 1-0. Crewe had Dennis Nelson sent off and lost the replay 1-0.

Ray Graydon spins away in triumph after scoring the only goal of the game during the Second Division home game against Blackpool at Villa Park on October 12, 1974. Chico Hamilton is about to join in the congratulations but it looks like the sat-on Sammy Morgan is going to be detained for a second or two! Graydon was to enter the season with 19 goals, one fewer than Brian Little.

Unmarked Chris Nicholl (left), with Brian Little and Ray Graydon in attendance, heads the second goal from a Jimmy Brown free-kick after only eight minutes of the crushing of York on December 14, 1974. Graydon (with his 17th of the season), Little and Chico Hamilton were also on target in a 4-0 win that left Villa sixth in the table, nine points adrift of Tommy Docherty's Manchester United, the leaders.

The Big Time Beckons

Villa's League Cup run took them past Hartlepool and Colchester before this semi-final pairing with Chester. The Division Four team held on for a draw at Sealand Road and went out on aggregate by the odd goal, celebrated here by Keith Leonard (left) and Brian Little. The win meant manager Ron Saunders had achieved the unique feat of going to the final three years in succession, with different clubs.

We're there again! Doug Ellis pours the champers for Chico Hamilton as (from left) Keith Leonard, Frank Carrodus and Jim Cumbes join in the indulgences following the tight squeeze against Chester. The 3-2 second-leg win at Villa Park in late January meant Saunders' men had a month and a half to prepare for their final clash with his former club Norwich, who beat Manchester United 3-2 on aggregate.

While Villa were preparing for Wembley in the League Cup, Fulham would be heading there in the FA Cup final in 1974-75. In the meantime, the clubs clashed in the League on February 8, 1975 and Brian Little went close with this header that was matched by a high-kicking goalline clearance by Alan Mullery. Also keeping guard is no 6 Bobby Moore. Villa had to come from behind for a 1-1 draw thanks to Chris Nicholl's goal.

Villa really had the promotion bit between their teeth when they avenged an earlier defeat at Old Trafford with a 2-0 victory against leaders Manchester United on February 22. Keeper Alex Stepney is relieved here to see Bobby McDonald's effort cleared off the line by Alex Forsyth but the resulting corner saw Charlie Aitken make it 2-0 in only the 24th minute. The also-pictured Ray Graydon had opened the scoring.

Winning at Wembley

Anxious moments beneath the twin towers for Villa as the falling Ted MacDougall pulls back a cross aimed for Phil Boyer with keeper Jim Cumbes out of position. Left-back Charlie Aitken and skipper Ian Ross are on the line just in case. Below: A section of Villa's massed support for their second appearance in the final in five seasons.

A brilliant save pushes the ball round the post from a header by Chris Nicholl (second from the right) as a tense League Cup final deadlock reaches into the last 12 minutes. Unfortunately for John Bond's Norwich, who like their opponents were a promotion-seeking Second Division outfit at the time, the stop came from defender Mel Machin and not from keeper Kevin Keelan - and a penalty was the obvious outcome.

Defining moment.....Ray Graydon can hardly miss as the ball drops kindly for him via Kevin Keelan's fine spot-kick save and then the upright. The winger's eagerly accepted second chance brought Villa their first piece of silverware for 14 years.

Now for the party….Chico Hamilton and young Scot Bobby MacDonald, with substitute Alun Evans in the background, milk the applause of the fans after Norwich had been defeated 1-0.

And the masses were out in force again when the team returned home with the cup to savour the obligatory open-top bus tour of the city.

Going up! Brian Little raises his fists in triumph as he scores one of the four goals which secured Villa's promotion via a 4-0 win over Sheffield Wednesday at Hillsborough. Villa, who had won 3-0 at Blackpool a few days earlier in front of some 10,000 travelling fans, finished three points behind champions Manchester United, with Norwich - a further five points adrift - also making the step up.

Sunderland's players sportingly provide a guard of honour to welcome Villa on to the pitch for the final home game of the memorable 1974-75 campaign. Dave Watson is the man nearest the camera as Ian Ross leads his team out after they ensured they were ending their eight-year exile from top-flight football. In front of more than 57,000, Villa gave themselves a fitting send-off by winning with two goals in the last 11 minutes. Sunderland just missed out on promotion by finishing fourth but went up the following year.

To cap a terrific 1974-75 season, the Villa players appeared (right) in the directors' box at the front of the main stand after the victory against Sunderland to salute followers who had backed them in huge numbers.

Below: Many a happy face in Villa's dressing room as well, as Ron Saunders - not a man given to great displays of emotion - joins his players to contemplate the calories they are about to pile on. Scouser John Gidman opts for liquid refreshment first - straight from the bottle of course!

Frank Carrodus, who played 196 matches in five years at Villa Park, twists his body to get a header in on goal during the first-round UEFA Cup away leg against Antwerp in the autumn of 1975. But the club's first-ever European tie was a miserable affair. The Belgians won this game 4-1 despite a goal by Ray Graydon and then extended their aggregate lead by winning 1-0 at Villa Park.

All singing, all dancing......the Holte End was a great place to be in the mid-to-late 1970s.

Close escape for Manchester United as they survive this attack, led by Brian Little and the falling Chris Nicholl, in the League Cup clash at Villa Park on October 8, 1975. Villa lost 2-1 and so relinquished their hold on the silverware they had picked up six months earlier. Life was proving taxing in the loftier surroundings and Ron Saunders soon invested £175,000 to land Dennis Mortimer from Coventry.

Ray Graydon goes into a celebratory leap in front of the Witton Lane fans after equalising against Southampton in an FA Cup third-round replay in January, 1976. But the Second Division Saints, whose defender Mel Blyth is powerless to prevent the ball going into the net, rallied to win in extra-time and stayed in the giant-killing mood to go all the way and beat Manchester United in the final.

A familiar pose from Andy Gray as he laps it up with fans after scoring past Alex Stepney and giving Villa a 2-1 victory in their Division One game against Manchester United on February 21, 1976. The Scot was already firing after moving south from Dundee United for £110,000 in September, 1975. But the side had slipped well below half-way in the table and immediate relegation became a threat.

What's that moving in the long grass? Andy Gray, Bobby McDonald, Ian Ross, Chico Hamilton, Brian Little and John Gidman are disconcerted by the hot breath of three Great Danes on their necks during pre-season training in 1976. Villa had finished 16th in the table the previous spring, a comfortable nine points above Wolves, who filled the highest of the relegation spots, just beneath Birmingham.

A Major Force

Andy Gray looks on approvingly as strike partner Brian Little fires home goal no 2 against visiting Manchester City in a one-sided League Cup tie on September 1, 1976. Asa Hartford, Mike Doyle and Villa's John Robson are the other players in the picture. Once more, the competition was to bring some very special times to Villa Park…..

Distressing scenes at what was intended as a convivial occasion - a supposedly friendly trip by Scottish giants Rangers to Villa Park in October, 1976. The game was abandoned soon after the interval when the pitch was invaded by visiting fans. More than 100 spectators were hurt and 50 were arrested - but Villa were soon cleared of any blame.

Everything gelled for Villa one golden night a couple of weeks before Christmas, 1976. They not only beat reigning champions Liverpool, they hammered them 5-1, all their goals coming in a wonderful first half. Above: Brian Little is about to be hugged by John Gidman and Andy Gray after a tremendous curling shot for no 4 that left Emlyn Hughes bemused. And Gray was on the score-sheet twice, along with John Deehan, the Scot completing the home tally with this header (below) from a Dennis Mortimer free-kick. It was the striker's 22nd goal of a season that wasn't yet half-way through, including two for Scotland, and a sign Villa were becoming a top-flight force.

Another Gray day! This time it's Leicester on the receiving end as a header is enough to give Villa victory in an FA Cup third-round tie at Filbert Street on January 10, 1977. The club were destined to reach the quarter-final of the competition before going out away to eventual winners Manchester United but it was the other domestic knockout which occupied their main thoughts.

Drop it if you dare! Andy Gray and John Deehan are frustrated for once as QPR's Black Country-born keeper Phil Parkes clings on to the ball during the 0-0 draw in the away first leg of the League Cup semi-final at Loftus Road on February 2, 1977. The Rangers defender standing guard is David Webb. Gray had scored Villa's goal when they were beaten 2-1 at the venue in the League the previous autumn.

Andy Gray, Dennis Mortimer and Bobby McDonald watch Alex Cropley curl a shot goalwards in Villa's 2-2 draw with Coventry in the winter of 1976-77. Gray and John Gidman netted for a side who were performing in front of a 40,000-plus crowd for the fourth game running. On this particular derby day, Mortimer and McDonald were both playing against their former clubs.

Knockout football remained very much on Villa's agenda when they staged this fifth-round FA Cup tie against Port Vale on February 26, 1977. Brian Little is pictured skilfully working the opening from which he fired home the second goal in a 3-0 victory that also featured strikes by Chris Nicholl and John Deehan. West Ham had been sent packing from Villa Park by the same score in the previous round.

Above: John Deehan stabs home Villa's opening goal in their League Cup semi-final return against QPR on February 16, 1977. The club had the scent of a third Wembley appearance in the competition in seven years as 'Dixie' netted twice in front of 48,429. But the Londoners, whose defender David Webb is a split second late with this challenge, drew 2-2 to take the game to a third game at Highbury.

Left: Deehan is submerged by delighted team-mates after his goal, with Andy Gray clenching a joyous and triumphant fist at fans on the Holte End while John Robson and Alex Cropley prepare to join the happy throng.

Tale of two keepers in the Villa v QPR League Cup semi-final marathon. Above: Despair for Rangers' West Midlands-born no 1 Phil Parkes. Below: Delight for John Burridge (left) as he shares with Brian Little the joy of Villa's eventual triumph. In the third meeting - at Highbury on February 22, 1977 - Burridge kept a clean sheet at one end and looked on as Little scored all three goals at the other. The striker netted ten goals in the League Cup journey, which earlier accounted for Manchester City, Norwich, Wrexham and Millwall.

A Familiar Feat

Above: Villa and Everton step into the Wembley glare for the 1977 League Cup final. Below: More a lap of appreciation than a lap of honour. In between the taking of the two pictures, little happened in a disappointing 0-0 draw as Villa - trying to become the first club to lift the cup three times - were left a shade deflated. But they still thanked their fans afterwards for their support.

Villa and Everton moved north to Hillsborough for their League Cup final replay four days later - and again they couldn't be separated. They drew 1-1 at the home of Sheffield Wednesday in front of 54,840, with Roger Kenyon - pictured here in pursuit of Andy Gray - putting Villa ahead with an 80th minute own goal on a night ex-Birmingham star Bob Latchford netted at the death for the Merseysiders.

Precious little separated Villa and Everton in their League Cup final epic, with this second replay at Old Trafford on April 13 coming a full month and a day after the first meeting. John Deehan (left) contests an even battle with Bob Latchford and Ken McNaught, the Everton defender who was later to join Villa. In a game that made up for some of the routine fare of the previous two meetings, no 8 Brian Little scored twice for a side who twice trailed and Chris Nicholl struck with a spectacular long-range left-foot shot. Little's winner came two minutes before the end of extra-time - on an evening when Villa had to do without the injured Andy Gray.

John Gidman, later to play for Manchester United, clears under pressure from Steve Coppell in the FA Cup quarter-final at Old Trafford on March 19, 1977. In front of 57,089, leg-weary Villa toiled hard against Tommy Docherty's side, who would lift the Cup at Wembley a couple of months later. Villa, having slogged through two League Cup final deadlocks, scored through Brian Little, only to go out 2-1.

Three days after finally overcoming Everton and qualifying for Europe, Villa found the energy to overcome Coventry in the League at Highfield Road. Ron Saunders' side were on a run of four wins in five First Division games when goals by Gordon Cowans, Brian Little and (above) John Deehan saw them home 3-2. Ex-Villa youngster Bobby McDonald suffers an inquisition by team-mate Brian Roberts.

John Deehan uses his head to force home Dennis Mortimer's troublesome free-kick from out on the left wing and give Villa maximum League points at home to Middlesbrough on April 5, 1977. The Solihull-born striker, who was to join Albion in 1979 after a Villa Park career of 139 first-team appearances and 51 goals, scored 13 times in 27 First Division matches that season.

Nicely balanced and with his eyes only on the net, Brian Little shoots on the turn from Dennis Mortimer's pass and scores Villa's second goal in their 2-1 home win over Tottenham on April 20, 1977. John Deehan, also pictured, got the other - his sixth in seven League games. The side were to finish with a 4-0 home victory over Albion and so secure a final fourth placing. The Spurs defender is Keith Osgood.

Villa's second UEFA Cup campaign was much happier than their first, their 1977-78 adventure starting with this thrashing of Turkish side Fenerbahce, who were thumped 4-0 at Villa Park before losing 2-0 on their home ground. It was the first European tie the Midlanders had ever won. Frank Carrodus is sent sprawling (above) in the home leg, which was settled by goals by John Deehan (2), Andy Gray and Brian Little. At the time, Villa were in and out with their League form, interspersing defeats against Manchester City and Everton among some useful victories.

Villa were locked in an ordinary run of away League form when they picked up a 1-1 draw at Leeds on October 5, 1977 despite this John Deehan miss. Gordon Cowans is the nearest player up in support while (from left) Gordon McQueen, Trevor Cherry and Paul Madeley are the harassed defenders. Villa cured their travel sickness by winning at Leicester on their next First Division trip, having preceded the visit to Elland Road with a victory over Wolves and a painful home defeat against Birmingham.

Above: Ken McNaught (right) punches the air in joy and finds no 9 Andy Gray just as eager to celebrate after the defender's first goal for Aston Villa. It came in the first leg of the UEFA Cup second-round clash with Gornik Zabrze on October 19, 1977, and was quickly followed by another from the same player. The former Everton man's brace saw the Poles off 2-0 on the night and meant Villa planted one foot in the next round.
Right: An unusual choice of pre-match gift as Villa skipper Frank Carrodus meets his counterpart before the return in foggy Poland. Saunders' men were comfortable enough in completing the task as Andy Gray's fine header earned them a 1-1 draw and saw them through on a 3-1 aggregate.

Another step along the UEFA Cup trail as Athletic Bilbao keeper Iribar fumbles Alex Cropley's right-wing corner into the net in the home first leg of the third-round tie on November 23, 1977. Ken McNaught is the white-shirted player closest to hand for a Villa side who won 2-0, John Deehan also scoring, and then drew 1-1 in the return in the Basque city thanks to Dennis Mortimer's goal.

Villa's proud reign as League Cup holders ended with this 4-2 defeat at Nottingham Forest in round four in November, 1977, after earlier victories over Exeter City and QPR. Goals by Brian Little and Frank Carrodus failed to save Villa, whose no 1 attacking threat Andy Gray is shut out here by Larry Lloyd. Brian Clough's Forest were to win the title and League Cup that season and the European Cup for the following two years.

UEFA Cup elimination came Villa's way on a stirring night at the Nou Camp on March 15, 1978. Following a 2-2 draw at home in the first leg, secured by late goals from Ken McNaught and John Deehan, Villa gave mighty Barcelona and a 90,000 crowd a scare despite the loss of John Gidman to a first-half sending-off. They opened the scoring in Spain through Brian Little while Deehan had his sights on another breakthrough as the ball just cleared the home bar (above left). Allan Evans and McNaught had Johan Cruyff and co perturbed and stretched in this incident (above right) and McNaught struck the bar before the players left the field (below).

Villa had won at Arsenal in their previous away League game but went down 1-0 at Birmingham in the follow-up on February 25, 1978. John Deehan is right out of luck here as, much to his and Frank Carrodus' disappointment, his flying header bounces back into play off the post. The relieved Blues defenders are Pat Howard and Joe Gallagher.

Ron Saunders is captured in pensive mood alongside Ron Bendall as they ponder the forthcoming season in August, 1978. The manager, a former England youth international striker with a career record of more than 200 goals, was half-way through his eight-year reign at the time. The Bendall family link with Villa ended following Doug Ellis' takeover in 1981.

Villa's class of 74-75 are reunited at a testimonial game in September, 1978 for Keith Leonard, the striker whose career had been ended prematurely by a knee injury. Leonard, in collar and tie, was honoured by the reappearance of the likes of Leighton Phillips, Steve Hunt, Jim Cumbes, Charlie Aitken, Chris Nicholl, Bobby McDonald, Ray Graydon, John Robson, Ian Ross and Frank Carrodus. Robson's football days had been curtailed by a more serious condition - multiple sclerosis.

More derby action as Allan Evans escapes Alistair Brown and flashes in the second-half equaliser against Albion at The Hawthorns in the 1-1 First Division draw on November 25, 1978. Brendon Batson swings and misses on the line while John Deehan, Len Cantello, Tony Godden and Derek Statham are also pictured. Albion briefly topped the table soon after this game - Gary Shaw's full League debut.

Derby Day Kings

Well done, my son! Brian Little, receives a congratulatory arm round the shoulder from Frank Carrodus as John Robson and Chico Hamilton move in to show their appreciation after the striker's goal at home to Birmingham on September 27, 1975. Little found life tougher following his 20 League goals the previous season but was to net 82 times for the club in 301 appearances.

The ups and downs of derby life. Brian Little, later to manage at The Hawthorns, and Albion duo John Wile (left) and Alan Merrick take a tumble as Chris Nicholl, Chico Hamilton and the Baggies' Ian Edwards keep their feet in the promotion showdown on Easter Saturday, 1975. Villa's 3-1 win came via three goals in eight minutes round the hour mark after Tony Brown had put their promotion rivals ahead.

Goalscorer John Deehan soars above Wolves' former Birmingham defender Colin Brazier to beat keeper Phil Parkes in the all-West Midlands clash at Villa Park on September 23, 1977. The other goal in the 2-0 win was put into his own net by Brazier. Villa had ensured themselves a final placing of eighth by the time they lost the return at Molineux 3-1 in the spring.

Trouble flares in a Villa v Albion clash on December 10, 1977 that was distinctly short on festive goodwill. No 9 Andy Gray and Frank Carrodus are among the peacemakers in this incident which has Albion's Len Cantello and Paddy Mulligan at its centre. Villa emerged from a barren sequence with a 3-0 win that was soured by a broken leg suffered by Alex Cropley in a challenge with Alistair Brown.

A crucial and characteristic goal for Andy Gray as he launches himself at the ball to score what proved to be the Villa winner in their floodlit derby at Coventry on March 21, 1978. Brian Little and Ken McNaught netted the others in a 3-2 victory that kept the club on the fringes of the race for a European place, although they didn't reach the heights of the previous season.

A winning start to 1978-79 for Villa as Andy Gray shakes off a challenge from no 5 Bob Hazell and beats Paul Bradshaw for the only goal of the derby at home to Wolves on kick-off day. Little did the 43,922 crowd know that the Scottish international striker would join Wolves for a then British record fee just over a year later. The also-pictured Brian Little was also to serve at Molineux, as a coach and caretaker manager.

Gordon Cowans is the toast of Villa Park following the goal that completed a League double over Birmingham on March 3, 1979. Andy Gray and Brian Little are quick to congratulate him on the strike that meant the side had recorded 1-0 victories over their neighbours home and away. The attendance numbered a more than healthy 42,419 despite the inclement conditions.

Stylish Sid.....Gordon Cowans again exudes composure and confidence as he wrongfoots Jeff Wealands to help Villa to a 2-1 win against Birmingham at St Andrew's on October 11, 1980. Cowans had also struck from the penalty spot at Old Trafford the week before in the first of two 3-3 draws that season between Villa and Manchester United.

Contrasting emotions for Birmingham keeper Jim Montgomery and Villa's Andy Gray as the ball bounces towards the net for the only goal of the Second City derby on October 21, 1978 - the visitors' first victory in six League games. Villa were involved at the time in a turbulent League Cup journey that took them past Sheffield United and Crystal Palace before they were surprisingly ousted by Luton.

Jimmy Rimmer shows his mastery in the air as he leaves his line to take the ball off the head of Bryan Robson in Villa's 2-1 First Division victory at Albion on February 24, 1980. Brian Little and no 5 Ken McNaught scored the winners' goals with (from left) Dennis Mortimer, Gordon Cowans and Gary Williams also in shot. The Baggies man next to Mortimer is ex-Vila favourite John Deehan.

Sights Set High

Left: Man for all requirements….John Gregory, destined to manage Villa two decades later, shows off the array of different positions he had already filled for the club by the autumn of 1978. The Mr Versatile of the squad cost £40,000 when signed from Northampton in 1977 and was to make 76 senior appearances for the club before moving on to Brighton, QPR, Derby and Portsmouth.

Below: Goal coming up - but perhaps not quite how it looks. Dennis Mortimer's full-length dive and header did not itself find the net in this League clash away to Everton at the end of January, 1979. But it did the next best thing as Gary Shelton closed in to nod home the rebound after keeper David Lawson's brilliant save. The defender on the right is Colin Todd.

Above: Bolton defender Paul Jones, under pressure from Andy Gray, gets airborne to net an embarrassing own goal in his team's 3-0 defeat at Villa Park on March 7, 1979. At a time when clubs were catching up on a hefty fixture backlog after a severe winter, Gray was also on the score-sheet, along with Kenny Swain, who is pictured to the right three months after his £100,000 arrival. It was the last leg of Villa's nine-game unbeaten League run.

Left: Another helping hand, this time gift-wrapped by Chelsea's Graham Wilkins, who receives a comforting arm from team-mate Micky Droy after an own goal on April 28, 1979. Villa had been trailing to a team already sure to be relegated but hit back for this 2-1 win - their fourth consecutive victory. Kenny Swain, a Chelsea player until that winter, had equalised for a Villa side who again finished eighth.

New season, new face.....Tony Morley whacks in Villa's winner from a free-kick in the home game against newly-promoted Brighton on August 22, 1979. The winger, signed that summer for £200,000 from Burnley, did not have much time to develop a partnership with Andy Gray, the striker joining Wolves in this month for a British record fee. Allan Evans scored the other goal in Villa's 2-1 victory.

Left: A proud Gary Shaw toasts a goal in the home victory against Bolton on November 3, 1979. Brian Little is first to join in the fun while Des Bremner celebrates behind them. On target as well in a 3-1 win were Allan Evans and Dennis Mortimer as Villa reached stage seven of a run of 11 League games without defeat.

Below: Doug Ellis states his case in calling for the removal as directors of Harry Kartz and the Bendalls, Ron and Donald, at a Villa Park EGM in November of 1979. Power struggles were part of club life and it was announced at the following night's AGM that Ellis' bid had just failed. Also pictured on the front row are (left to right) Eric Houghton, Steve Stride, president Trevor Gill, Kartz, Ron Bendall and Donald Bendall.

It's a bit tricky down at the deep end! Dennis Mortimer and Gary Owen watch David Geddis and John Wile aquaplane to a halt on a sodden surface during the Villa v Albion derby on October 13, 1979. The goalless draw underlined the scoring shortage Ron Saunders' side were going through at the time, Villa failing to come up with a goal in six games out of eight.

Disappointment for Andy Gray as he is beaten to a loose ball by England keeper Peter Shilton in this late 1970s clash with Nottingham Forest. Martin O'Neill, no 7 John Deehan and Brian Little are the bystanders on a day when East Midlands mastered West Midlands. Forest won two European Cups, a League title and a host of other honours and Villa would soon be following them along the glory trail.

No mistake from Allan Evans as he sidefoots a penalty past Roger Jones in Villa's 2-1 home win over Stoke on November 17, 1979. It came two minutes from the end but there was still time for Stoke's Denis Smith to be sent off. Evans, signed from Dunfermline for £30,000 in 1977, started as a striker and retained his scoring knack after becoming a defender, giving Villa 12 years' terrific service.

All power and determination, Ken McNaught climbs above Tommy Caton to power a header goalwards as Dennis Mortimer looks on. This unrewarded effort in a 2-2 draw with Manchester City came on February 27, 1980, Gary Shaw and a Willie Donachie own goal making up the home tally. City's no 2 is Ray Ranson, the full-back who was much later to be linked with an attempted purchase of Villa.

Villa and West Ham players, clad in black armbands, observe a minute's silence in memory of late Football League secretary Alan Hardaker before their FA Cup quarter-final meeting on March 8, 1980. Nearest the camera is Hammers' England midfielder Trevor Brooking. Villa's day became even sadder as they lost 1-0 to a side then in the Second Division.

Geoff Palmer and Paul Bradshaw frustrate Villa - in particular Allan Evans - in the home clash with Wolves on March 10, 1980. The visitors, captained by Emlyn Hughes (right), won 3-1 despite a Gary Shaw goal and used the game for Andy Gray to serve a suspension so he could play in the League Cup final against Nottingham Forest five days later. Gray, who had become Britain's most expensive footballer when leaving Villa for £1,469,000, certainly made an impact at Wembley, netting the only goal with a tap-in.

Tony Morley (right) was the man on target when Villa drew 1-1 at home to Ipswich on March 22, 1980 to end an unhappy sequence of three consecutive defeats. Ron Saunders' men still ended a satisfactory seventh in the table and so hint further that success was on the way. Also pictured are Gordon Cowans and Midlands-born keeper Paul Cooper.

Left: No slips from Cowans as he sidefoots a penalty beyond the dive of Jim Blyth to add to Colin Gibson's goal and put Villa into an unassailable 2-0 lead in their First Division win over Coventry at Highfield Road on April 29, 1980. Villa won 2-1 and climbed to fifth as a result, finishing the season one spot higher than 12 months earlier.

Villa won the FA Youth Cup twice in nine seasons during the club's renaissance years but were out of luck in between when beaten 1-0 by Crystal Palace in this final staged at neutral Highbury in 1978. Brendan Ormsby is seen challenging Palace keeper Fry at the end of a run in which Villa had accounted for Nuneaton, Tottenham, Southampton, Grimsby and Burnley.

Villa's cubs enjoy their evening in the spotlight as they savour the feat of winning the FA Youth Cup in 1979-80. Robert Hopkins shows off the silverware after his side had held on for a 3-2 aggregate success despite visitors Manchester City's 1-0 victory in this Villa Park second leg of the final. Villa, who included Noel Blake, Paul Birch and Mark Walters, had won 3-1 at Maine Road with Trevor Ames scoring a hat-trick.

The Golden Era

The seeds of the title success are sewn.....Gary Shaw fires in the only goal in Villa's first home League game of their 1980-81 championship-winning season. Norwich, in particular centre-half Kevin Bond, are on the receiving end from a team who had kicked off their campaign with a 2-1 success at Leeds. Dennis Mortimer looks on approvingly at the young striker's late winner.

David Geddis rises in glorious isolation to head Villa's winner in their First Division derby at home to Wolves on September 20, 1980. An own goal by Emlyn Hughes (left) had set the side up for this first of three successive League victories after their previous two games had brought defeats against Ipswich and Everton. Allan Evans and Wolves pair George Berry and Geoff Palmer are also pictured.

It's a derby-day winner as Birmingham are left floundering by a sweet 84th minute strike from Allan Evans which Gary Shaw is ready to acclaim. This October 11 success at St Andrew's, also featuring a Gordon Cowans penalty, came three days after a trio of consecutive victories had been ended by a thrilling 3-3 draw away to Manchester United. Villa had also lost twice in their first 11 games - at home to Everton and away to an Ipswich side destined to emerge as serious title rivals.

Tony Morley terrorised the Tottenham defence in this comfortable 3-0 home victory on October 18, 1980. Morley is pictured here in the build-up to one of his two goals, Peter Withe netting the other for a side who were in the middle of a run of eight wins in nine League matches. In the middle of the three Spurs players is the former Villa man Gordon Smith.

Still firing, still winning....Gary Shaw beats the outstretched leg of the familiar figure of Steve Foster, a defender later to play for Villa, to complete the 4-1 rout of visiting Brighton on October 22, 1980. Dennis Mortimer, Des Bremner and Peter Withe also scored for a side who were recording their third successive League victory - and were also to win their next two.

Shaw on the mark again, this time with a header that helped see off Norwich 3-1 at Carrow Road on November 12, 1980 and so complete a League double over the Canaries. Shaw had a double of his own in the form of a match-winning brace, with Allan Evans netting the other goal. Villa subsequently encountered hitches and failed to win any of their next four First Division matches.

Winter is closing in as Tony Morley gets airborne to power home Villa's goal in their 1-1 home draw with Arsenal on November 29, 1980. In the absence of David O'Leary, Steve Walford is the Gunners no 6 while Graham Rix looks on from behind Gary Shaw. Villa, who had suffered the shock of going out of the League Cup away to Second Division Cambridge, were to have a crucial return clash with Arsenal on the last day of the season…..

Another derby-day triumph over the Blues is in the offing as David Geddis, a striker bought from Ipswich for £300,000 the previous season, is mobbed by his team-mates after scoring one of his two goals in a straightforward 3-0 home victory on December 13, 1980. Fellow striker Gary Shaw netted the other and the club seemed to be over a dodgy spell of four League games without a win.

David Geddis, one of the bit-part players as Villa astonishingly used only 14 players in their magnificent 1980-81 season, heads clear in the 2-2 draw at Nottingham Forest two days after Christmas. The striker, covered by Gary Williams, Allan Evans and Des Bremner, scored one of the goals on a day an own goal by the also-pictured Larry Lloyd kept Villa on track a week after they had lost at Brighton.

Villa had the scent of the big time in their nostrils when they brought down mighty Liverpool in this League clash on January 10, 1981. The lion on the Trinity Road stand roof provides a fitting backdrop as Peter Withe shakes off Colin Irwin to dispatch the opener past Ray Clemence and Alan Kennedy. Dennis Mortimer's goal completed a 2-0 win against the reigning champions and Villa were on their way.

A goal for Peter Withe in the thrilling 3-3 draw with Manchester United on March 14, 1981. Withe scored two and Shaw one in front of an enthralled crowd of over 42,000. It was Villa's tenth successive League game without defeat - and the championship juggernaut was gathering momentum. No 5 Ken McNaught, Allan Evans and Shaw are the other Villa men pictured while United's keeper is Gary Bailey. Coincidentally, it was the second draw between the clubs by that score that season.

David Geddis punches the air and acclaims the Holte End after his winner against Southampton on March 28, 1981. The goal followed one by Tony Morley and put Villa on their way to a 2-1 victory after a defeat at Tottenham the previous weekend. Geddis made only nine Football League appearances in the season but made them count by scoring four goals. The half-hidden Saints man is former Villa defender Chris Nicholl.

Above: The last of Villa's goals in their exhilarating 4-2 victory at Leicester on April 4, 1981 - a classic finish from Tony Morley. It was one of 12 goals the winger scored that season. Villa had lost just one of 13 League games and were within touching distance of domestic football's biggest prize.

Left: Albion proved tough Villa Park opponents under the famous lights on April 8, with Cyrille Regis - later to join Villa - and Remi Moses harassing Gordon Cowans and Allan Evans. A late goal by Peter Withe settled it.

Below: Oops! The night when it looked like going wrong.....Gary Shaw's goal here is merely a consolation in a game Villa lost 2-1 to arch-rivals Ipswich on April 14. The East Anglians were managed at the time by Bobby Robson.

Villa came up with a convincing response to the blow of the Ipswich defeat when they beat Nottingham Forest 2-0 four days later. Gordon Cowans had missed his previous penalty, against Tottenham, but made no mistake here as he sent Peter Shilton the wrong way. Forest had won the European Cup for the previous two seasons but were downed in this game as their old boy, Peter Withe, also got on target.

Two days after the revitalising win over Forest, Easter Monday brought mixed fortunes for Villa as they managed only a 1-1 draw at Stoke despite this fine Peter Withe goal. The striker, having just been named the club's player of the year, gets above Brendan O'Callaghan as Mike Doyle and Allan Evans look on at close quarters and Kenny Swain watches from a distance.

Villa signed off in front of their home fans in style on April 25, 1981, when they won 3-0 against a Middlesbrough side from whom they then hoped for a major helping hand the following weekend. Peter Withe is pictured getting airborne to head his team's second goal after Gary Shaw had broken the deadlock. Allan Evans was also on the score-sheet on a day Villa recorded the 16th victory of their 21-match home League programme.

It all boiled down to May 2, 1981, the last afternoon of the season, which took Villa on the difficult trip to third-placed Arsenal. Ipswich were the only side who could pip Ron Saunders' men to the crown, and all games were to kick off at 3pm on a Saturday, there being no live TV coverage of League matches in those days. Today's younger fans will also be surprised to know that Ipswich - away to Middlesbrough - also had a home match against Southampton still to come. It was a dramatic finish from which Villa knew a point would be enough - good reason for their 16,000 ticket allocation to be snapped up in double quick time. It is estimated they actually had some 20,000 followers inside Highbury, where £3 tickets were changing hands for £20.

For a side who had been terrific all season, Villa performed dismally at Highbury and were 2-0 down by half-time, with (from left) Peter Withe, Des Bremner, Kenny Swain and former Gunners keeper Jimmy Rimmer powerless to keep out this effort from Willie Young for goal no 2. Brian McDermott also scored and, with the title dream in big danger of turning into a nightmare as the second half failed to produce a goal, Villa found themselves requiring a favour from almost 300 miles away. Thankfully, Middlesbrough obliged by beating Ipswich at Ayresome Park, confirmation of which finally came through on Highbury's packed south bank and sparked jubilant scenes among the masses (below).

Some Villa supporters spilled on to their pitch in their exuberance and caused tense looks on faces of bystanders near the entrance to the tunnel. The players, meanwhile, were already having a party of their own in the safety of the dressing-room (below), where Allan Evans and Dennis Mortimer were well to the fore, with Des Bremner and Tony Morley joining in the fun behind them..

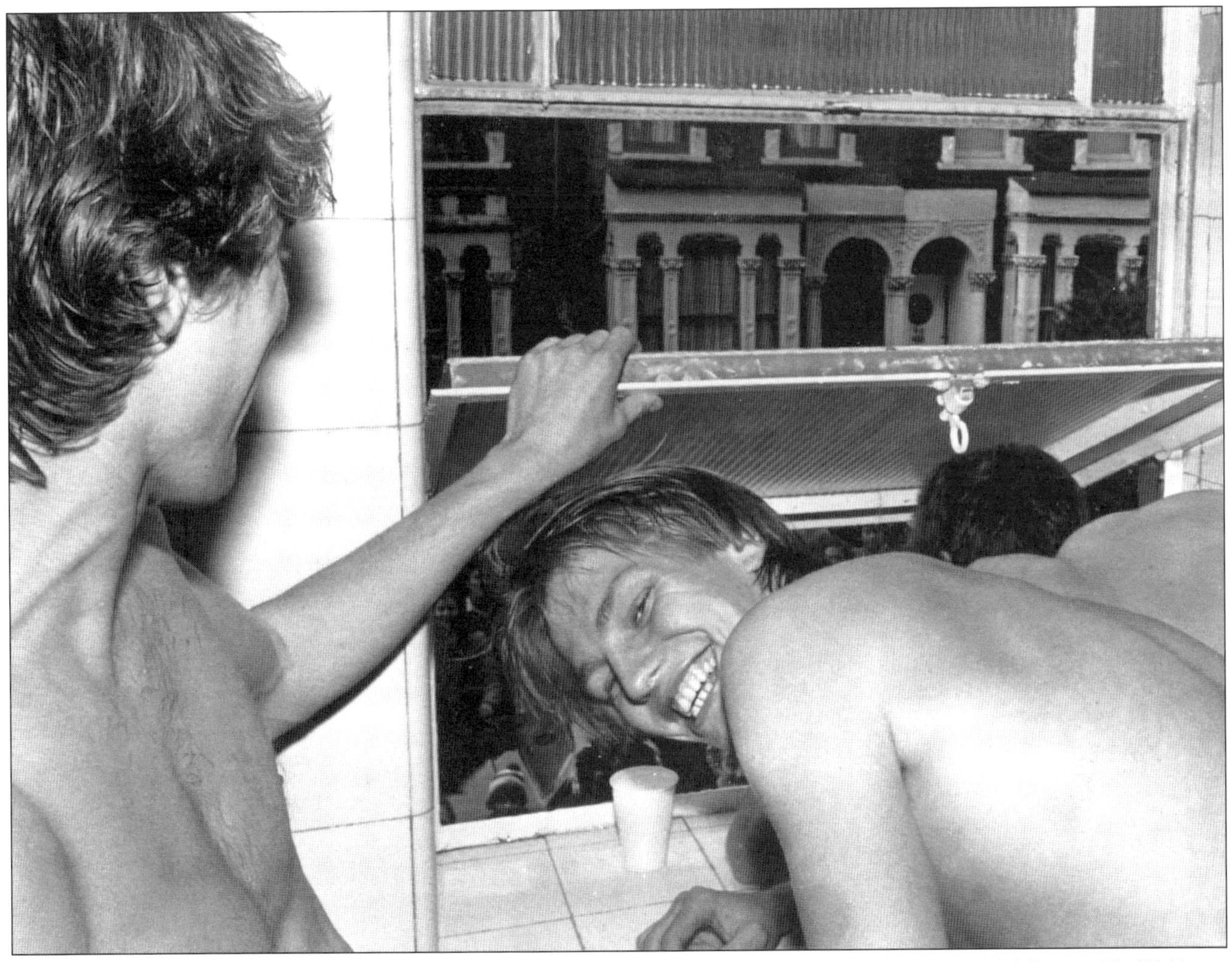

Watching you watching us.....Gordon Cowans (left) helps Gary Shaw take a peek at the Villa supporters rejoicing outside Highbury. Cowans was one of an astonishing seven players who played in every one of Villa's 46 League and cup games that season. The others were Jimmy Rimmer, Kenny Swain, Ken McNaught, Dennis Mortimer, Des Bremner and Tony Morley.

The title-winning celebrations were not restricted to only one day. For those with claret and blue blood, the elation lasted a lot longer than that. The fans turned out in predictably huge numbers when the squad returned to the city and took a tour of honour aboard an open-top bus. It was Villa's first championship success for 71 long years since 1910.

Gary Shaw, scorer of 18 goals along the road to glory, looks down in some awe (above) on the throng of supporters in Birmingham's Chamberlain Square............and Ron Saunders takes his turn (below) in showing off the League Championship trophy. The manager was to shock the football world by quitting the following February and joining arch-rivals Birmingham.

After the heroics came the plaudits. Brian Clough and Jimmy Greaves offer their congratulations to Ron Saunders, 20-goal leading scorer Peter Withe (Midlands Player of the Year) and Young Player of the Year Gary Shaw later in the Bank Holiday weekend. Brian Little, not part of the title-winning squad and his career curtailed by injury, received a special award for his services to football.

Villa were looking forward to their first taste of the European Cup when the new offices in the North Stand opened in the summer of 1981. Steve Stride (left), who had become the top flight's youngest secretary in 1979 and who remains in the post today as well as on the club's board, shares a word with Kenny Swain, one of the cornerstones of Villa's finest season for many decades.

A hair-raising experience for David Geddis as he challenges Tottenham keeper Ray Clemence for a high ball in Villa's Charity Shield clash with FA Cup winners Spurs at Wembley in August, 1981. The sides shared the trophy by drawing 2-2 in front of 92,445, Peter Withe and Falco each scoring twice. It was the fourth time Villa had contested the Charity Shield. When they faced Manchester City in 1972, it was as Third Division champions.

More action from the twin towers captures Allan Evans in animated pose between the Spurs duo of Graham Roberts (left) and Mark Falco.

Villa's proudly acquired Championship crown tilted uneasily on the very first day of their defence. Newly-promoted Notts County, humbled in a final midweek warm-up game, were seen as lambs to the slaughter on the opening afternoon of 1981-82 but sprung a shock with a deserved 1-0 victory. Here, Colin Gibson watches Ken McNaught challenge debutant Magpies winger John Chiedozie.

Peter Withe climbs above Stoke keeper Peter Fox, who turns his back in unorthodox style, to open the scoring in the Midlands derby on September 23, 1981. The burly centre-forward later struck again but the Potteries side, also represented in this picture by (from left) Mickey Thomas, Sammy McIlroy and Brendan O'Callaghan, hit back for a 2-2 draw that extended the champions' faltering start.

Allan Evans stoops as Jimmy Rimmer leaves his line to take a cross off the head of Bolton's Neil Whatmore at Villa Park on September 26, 1981. Frank Worthington is the visiting forward lurking to the left. The 0-0 draw meant title holders Villa had won only one of their first seven fixtures in the League and that run was to stretch to only one win in nine - a 3-1 victory at Tottenham.

This game did go right for Villa, much to the despair of troubled West Midlands rivals Wolves. The Molineux men were lurching towards relegation and near financial oblivion by the time they were beaten 3-0 on October 24, 1981, a Gary Shaw brace and Geoff Palmer own goal making up the tally. Palmer bows his head after his howler, with Shaw and his team-mates too embarrassed to celebrate.

Villa and Notts County clashed three times in 1981-82, with contrasting results. Newly-promoted Notts, having recorded a shock Villa Park win on the opening day, completed an unlikely double by the same score in this January return at Meadow Lane, where Des Bremner and Gary Williams are seen closing in on Gordon Mair. Just before this wintry meeting, though, Villa ran out handsome 6-0 winners in a delayed FA Cup third-round tie at County, with David Geddis scoring four.

Peter Withe watches his header beat Ray Clemence for the equaliser against Tottenham on February 17, 1982. The goal, witnessed by Ken McNaught, earned Villa a 1-1 draw four days after they had lost 1-0 in an FA Cup fifth-round tie at Spurs. Ron Saunders had resigned eight days earlier after claiming Ron Bendall's board had altered his contract.

Tense moments in the derby at St Andrew's on February 20, 1982 as Jimmy Rimmer reaches through the legs of Peter Withe to grab the ball in a congested area. Allan Evans, Des Bremner and a grounded Ken McNaught are close at hand to ensure Birmingham's attackers go no further. Withe scored for the third successive League game to give Villa a 1-0 victory. Sensationally, Saunders took over as Blues manager two days later.

The trusty right foot of Gary Shaw does the trick once more as Coventry are put to the sword at Villa Park on February 27, 1982. Villa won 2-1, with Gordon Cowans netting the other goal from the penalty spot. Garry Thompson, destined to swap sky blue for Albion's navy blue and then the claret and blue, is in the middle of the trio of visiting players in the background.

The clincher! Although Villa's League form was disappointing, they were making great strides in Europe, underlined here as Ken McNaught heads Gordon Cowans' corner past keeper Victor Chanov to give Villa a 2-0 second-leg victory over Soviet champions Dynamo Kiev in the European Cup quarter-final. The sides had drawn 0-0 behind the Iron Curtain. Peter Withe was close to netting this one himself but was happy enough to see the centre-half and Gary Shaw take the scoring honours on another memorable night.

New face at the helm….Tony Barton, initially appointed only on a caretaker basis, gets the message across to his players in this chilly, but relaxed training-ground scene on March 19, 1982. It was two days after the defeating of Dynamo Kiev and the morning Villa learned that Belgian giants Anderlecht would be their European Cup semi-final opponents.

Happiness is a goal for the Villa. Tony Morley and scorer David Geddis acclaim this strike in front of the Holte End, with Gary Williams about to add his congratulations. But First Division success was thin on the ground for the club in 1981-82 as they trailed in an underwhelming 11th, with Liverpool regaining their mantel as champions. It was to the continent that Villa looked in search of glory.....

Villa were proving a huge hit on the other side of the English Channel. Having thrashed Icelanders Valur, then edged past Dynamo Berlin on the away goals rule, they followed up their conquest of Kiev by beating Anderlecht 1-0 in the first leg of the semi-final. Tony Morley, who had scored twice away to Berlin, one of them a memorable goal of the season effort, gave them the narrow lead they took with them from Elmdon out to Belgium.

Champions of Europe

Gary Shaw is out of luck with an overhead kick as he attempts to give his side the breathing space of a second goal away to Anderlecht on April 21, 1982. The game remained deadlocked at 0-0 but that was good enough for Villa to reach their first European final.

Job done....Allan Evans and Pat Heard, show off souvenir Anderlecht shirts after Villa booked their ticket to the biggest club game on the Continent. Also in the happy group are Gordon Cowans, Des Bremner, Gary Williams, Gary Shaw, Kenny Swain and Ken McNaught.

Villa were certainly underdogs when they set foot in the Feyenoord Stadium in Rotterdam on May 27, 1982. Opponents Bayern Munich boasted not only the richer pedigree - they had won the handsome European Cup in three successive years in the mid-1970s - but had also had a more successful domestic campaign. Villa often had their backs to the wall in the Dutch port and it was something of a surprise when Tony Morley (above) escaped the German shackles to set up what proved to be an untidy winning goal for Peter Withe mid-way through the second half. The winger was quick (left) to try the silverware for size when it came to the lap of honour in the company of Gary Shaw.

Peter Withe left Nottingham Forest for Villa before Brian Clough's side won the competition in consecutive years but achieved the crowning moment of his career by ensuring Europe's biggest prize came to England for a remarkable sixth year in succession; that despite the early loss of keeper Jimmy Rimmer through injury, young Nigel Spink going on in his place.

Here we are again! For the second May in a row, Birmingham's Chamberlain Square was handed over to thousands of Villa fans, this time in celebration of European Cup glory. Dennis Mortimer (right) had also skippered the club to the title but Tony Barton (left) must have been pinching himself. His tag as caretaker manager had been upgraded to that of permanent boss only a few weeks earlier.

Back Down To Earth

Peter Withe lashes in one of the goals by which Villa overcame the East German national side 4-2 in a pre-season friendly. in the summer of 1981. As well as defeating Bayern Munich in the final of the European Cup, the club had also been on a three-match tour of Germany in 1980-81, winning one, drawing one and losing one of their three games.

Gordon Cowans gets horizontal to head Villa in front at home to Sunderland on kick-off day, 1982. But, just as against Notts County as League champions 12 months earlier, a side of whom much was expected were to fall flat on their faces against unfancied opposition - this time in a 3-1 defeat. Villa's start quickly became much worse with defeats at Everton (5-0) and Southampton.

Dennis Mortimer takes careful aim and scores the goal that lifted the sudden Villa Park gloom. After three opening League defeats, Tony Barton's side embarked on a run of victories by trouncing Luton 4-1 here on September 8, 1982. Mal Donaghy is the visiting defender closest to making a challenge. This success was soon followed by wins at home to Nottingham Forest and away to Manchester City.

An unusual backdrop to the launch of Villa's European Cup defence as Dennis Mortimer bursts between two Besiktas players at a deserted stadium on September 16, 1982. Mortimer, Peter Withe and Tony Morley scored to give the home side a 3-1 win on an afternoon when fans were barred as a result of crowd disturbances at the tie in Anderlecht the previous spring. The second leg in Turkey was drawn.

A falling Gary Shaw, backed up as usual by strike partner Peter Withe, sees an effort clear the angle by inches as Villa look to add to their tally in the home clash with Swansea on September 25, 1982. Goals by Dennis Mortimer and Allan Evans nevertheless gave the side a 2-0 win - their fourth successive League victory following an alarming first fortnight.

Villa's fortunes as European Cup holders remained patchy, although this crushing 4-0 Villa Park win over Tottenham on October 30, 1982, provided a bright spot. Gary Shaw expresses his delight after completing the rout, which also featured goals by Gordon Cowans (two) and Tony Morley. The side were victorious as well in their next three home matches during a campaign which remained hot and cold.

Mark Walters, a new kid on the block in the wake of the club's glory years, is unlucky with this shot in the 1-1 draw at home to Ipswich on December 29, 1982. It was left to Peter Withe to score the goal that earned Villa a point. Walters, a former England schoolboy and youth international who was then only 18, was to play more than 700 matches for his various clubs and win a single full England cap.

Gary Williams can't believe it as Manchester City survive further damage on their League visit to Villa Park on January 22, 1983. And the miss became more expensive when City, trailing at the time to a Gary Shaw goal, hit back for a point from a 1-1 draw. Williams played 21 games in the title-winning campaign of 1980-81 and upped his appearance rate with 28 in 1981-82 and 35 in 1982-83.

Ken McNaught found himself squarely in the spotlight when Villa, beaten in the World Club Championship by Penarol in Tokyo the previous month, added the Super Cup to their haul on January 26, 1983. Trailing 1-0 to Barcelona from the first leg at the Nou Camp, they gained revenge over the Spanish giants for their UEFA Cup exit at their hands in 1977-78 by winning 3-0 at Villa Park. Gary Shaw equalised on aggregate only 11 minutes from time and then, in extra-time, Gordon Cowans (penalty) put them in front. Finally, McNaught took off (above) to complete a 3-1 aggregate victory. The defender also had the honour of collecting the silverware (left) because skipper Allan Evans had been sent off on a night on which Barca had Alberto and Marcos dismissed.

A hit and a miss for Villa from the home leg of their European Cup quarter-final clash with Juventus on March 2, 1983. Above: Gordon Cowans steams in to equalise a goal the Italian champions had scored after only 43 seconds. But the visitors regained the lead and held on for a precious 2-1 first-leg lead despite this determined assault on their goal by Peter Withe (below). The crowd was more than 45,000.

Tony Barton and his players prepare to step aboard for their flight to Turin for the daunting second leg of their European Cup showdown against Juventus. And it was in northern Italy that the club's hold on the trophy was finally broken with a 3-1 defeat in front of a crowd of more than 66,000. That spelled elimination on a 5-2 aggregate around the same time that Villa's FA Cup hopes were sunk at Arsenal, also at the last-eight stage.

A leg-up for Eamonn Deacy from Gordon Cowans after the Irishman had brilliantly scored one of the three goals by which Villa condemned Norwich to an odd-goal Villa Park defeat on March 5, 1983. Deacy, nursing a cut and bandaged left knee, was joined on the score-sheet by the old firm of Withe and Shaw, and found no 6 Dennis Mortimer and Des Bremner descending on him quickly for the congratulations.

Gary Shaw, Villa's top marksman in 1982-83, didn't score any easier goals than this one against Coventry on March 19, 1983. It was made by Dennis Mortimer on the right and set the side up for a 4-0 win in which Peter Withe (2) and Allan Evans also netted. Les Sealey, later of Villa, is the Sky Blues keeper and Gerry Francis the player biting the dust. It was Villa's fifth win in six League games.

Villa produced a winning final flourish to a chequered season when beating Arsenal 2-1 on May 14, 1983. Helped on their way by this goal from Gary Shaw, with Dennis Mortimer joining the ball in the net, Tony Barton's side secured a respectable finish of sixth, with Graham Taylor's Watford emerging as unlikely runners-up to Liverpool. Colin Gibson also netted for Villa, who were unbeaten at home in the League from December and so made it back into Europe in the UEFA Cup. David O'Leary was in the visitors' line-up.

Gordon Cowans shares a joke with 'Big Ron' after being presented with the Midlands Footballer of the Year award in May, 1983. The midfielder played all 57 Villa games in the League, domestic cups, Europe and World Club Championship, managing a double-figure goal tally. His world fell apart, though, when he suffered a badly broken leg in the following pre-season and sat out the entire 1983-84 programme.

In Decline

Nigel Spink was the new 'safe hands' of Villa Park by the time of this pre-season clash at Birmingham in August, 1983. It was time for the younger man to be given his opportunity following Jimmy Rimmer's free-transfer switch to Swansea, the ex-Manchester United and Arsenal keeper having barely missed a game during a Villa appearances haul of almost 290 since his arrival in 1977. Billy Wright and Mick Harford are the challenging Blues players.

Peter Withe lets fly (above) with a fierce shot that fails to find the target in Villa's second game of 1983-84. It didn't matter too much as Mark Walters gave the club a 1-0 win over Sunderland on August 29, two days after a thrilling 4-3 home victory over Ron Wylie's Albion. At Withe's side is the ex-Coventry midfielder Andy Blair, of whom more was now expected in Cowans' absence.

Mark Walters takes evasive action as Wolves midfielder Kenny Hibbitt moves across to challenge in the 1-1 First Division One draw between the West Midlands rivals at Molineux on October 23, 1983. It was the first time a League fixture involving Villa was screened live on TV, the club having beaten visiting Birmingham 1-0 the previous weekend. The following Saturday, though, brought a nightmare 6-2 Villa Park hammering by Arsenal.

With Ken McNaught already at West Brom, Tony Morley set to follow and Jimmy Rimmer having moved to Swansea after remaining an ever-present no fewer than four times, Villa's League and European Cup winning squad were being dismantled by the time of this UEFA Cup KO by Spartak Moscow on November 2, 1983. After beating Vitoria Guimaraes, Villa took the lead against the Soviets with this Peter Withe header but lost 2-1 on the night after a 2-2 first-leg draw. It was their last European tie for seven years.

Nigel Spink dives in bravely as Gary Owen flies over him in Villa's 3-1 defeat at Albion on January 14, 1984. Dennis Mortimer and Des Bremner lend support to the keeper, with Garry Thompson and Cyrille Regis - both later to play for Villa - on the warpath on a day on which they shared Albion's goals. Gary Shaw scored for Villa, who were in a dismal run of six League games without a win.

Kevin Ratcliffe and Derek Mountfield - the latter destined to ply his trade at Villa Park - watch Peter Withe, a boyhood Everton fan, go crashing in Villa's League Cup semi-final first leg at Goodison on February 15, 1984. The Midlanders lost 2-0 before winning 1-0 in the second leg with a Paul Rideout goal. Villa had beaten Portsmouth, Manchester City, Albion and Norwich in the earlier rounds.

Peter Withe drives home the second of Villa's four goals, without reply, against relegation-bound Wolves on February 25, 1984. The crowd was a paltry 18,257 despite the side's encouraging draw at Arsenal the previous weekend. Wolves' keeper is former Villa man John Burridge while Alan Curbishley (left) is the team-mate up in closest support of the scorer.

A famous much-loved Aston Villa figure - in enemy colours! Paul McGrath, playing here for Manchester United, displays his customary poise and strength to fend off an advance from Paul Rideout in Villa's 3-0 home defeat on March 3, 1984. Villa had won 2-1 away to Ron Atkinson's team earlier in the season thanks to a Peter Withe brace and had swooped to recruit Steve Foster from Brighton shortly before this return.

It's all in an extraordinary night's work for Peter Withe as he shows his versatility in Villa's 3-3 derby draw away to Coventry on March 13, 1984. Above: The Holte End hero carries out his more familiar duties as he takes off to head his side's second goal. Below: Following the departure of Nigel Spink through concussion, he is pressed into action as an emergency goalkeeper but can do nothing to prevent Terry Gibson hitting the Sky Blues' final equaliser. Allan Evans (penalty) and Paul Rideout scored Villa's other goals.

Allan Evans heads away from Garry Birtles under the eye of Mervyn Day and Alan Curbishley in Villa's 1-0 home League win over Nottingham Forest on March 17, 1984. Day was starting a regular run in the club's goal and was to play 33 games for them in total before moving on. Steve McMahon netted the only goal but it didn't save Tony Barton from the sack in the summer after a final placing of tenth.

Graham Turner had been whisked in from Shrewsbury as manager by the time this fine Peter Withe header gave Villa the opening goal in their 4-2 home win over Chelsea on September 8, 1984. The side started the Turner era with two victories before crashing 3-0 at Newcastle and 5-0 at home to Nottingham Forest. Steve Foster, Paul Rideout and Withe (again) netted the other goals against Chelsea.

Under an apt advertisement - after all, he was the brains of Villa's midfield for years - the fit-again Gordon Cowans takes advantage of Paul Cooper's parry to a Colin Gibson shot and puts Villa ahead in their 2-1 home League win over Ipswich on February 2, 1985. The side were to finish tenth in Graham Turner's first season in charge, which ended with Cowans and Paul Rideout joining Italian club Bari for a combined £850,000. The gate here for Villa's third straight win was just 15,051.

Carlton Palmer looks on as Mark Walters sweeps Villa's second goal across the Hawthorns snow and ushers Albion to the Milk Cup exit on November 27, 1985. It was the decider in a 2-1 fourth-round win after the sides had drawn 2-2 at Villa Park. Earlier in the competition, Villa had beaten Exeter 12-2 on aggregate, Simon Stainrod scoring five, and won 3-0 at Leeds. They eventually lost in the semi-final to an Oxford side destined to lift the cup.

It was a sign of football's troubles at the time, especially in the West Midlands, that only 18,796 watched this 1-1 draw between Villa and visiting Albion on December 28, 1985. Paul Kerr swings his left foot to beat Alistair Robertson and Jimmy Nicholl for the opening goal, only for the Baggies - who had been beaten 3-0 in the earlier League meeting at The Hawthorns - to conjure up a late equaliser through ex-Villa midfielder Steve Hunt. The no 9 is Simon Stainrod.

Andy Gray, signed in 1985 for a second Villa stint that he perhaps came to regret, finishes with a flourish at the expense of former Birmingham keeper Tony Coton in the 4-1 home win over Watford on April 12, 1986. Tony Dorigo, Allan Evans (penalty) and Simon Stainrod scored the other goals for a side who finished in a disappointing 16th place. Albion and Blues fared worse and were relegated.

Down and Up

Simon Stainrod drives in his and Villa's second goal in the 2-0 home League win over Leicester on November 1, 1986. The victory came too late to save the skin of Graham Turner, though. He had been sacked earlier in the autumn and replaced by Celtic legend Billy McNeill with the club already entrenched in a battle to stay up. Tony Daley, Garry Thompson and Steve Hodge are the other Villa players pictured.

No way through for Paul Elliott as John Lukic gets just enough of the ball to deny him in Arsenal's 4-0 top-flight win at Villa Park on November 29, 1986. At the time, Villa were in a win-less sequence of seven League victories, although they made decent progress in the Littlewoods Cup before losing at Southampton. David O'Leary was a Gunners player at the time.

Relegation was close when Villa beat near neighbours Coventry 1-0 (right) in this meeting in the Second City on March 28, 1987. Paul Birch's goal brought maximum points a week after Villa had been humiliated to the tune of 5-0 at Southampton and a few days after a midweek 1-1 draw at home to Watford. Cyrille Regis is the Sky Blues player in the middle of the picture and Martin Keown the Villa man to the left.

A miserable run-in finally condemned Villa to Second Division football for the first time in 12 years - and cost Billy McNeill his job. Five years after the winning of the European Cup, the club finished bottom, eight points from safety, and went down in the company of Manchester City and Leicester. Below: Mark Walters taps in the equaliser in the 1-1 draw at Leicester on April 11, 1987, much to the disappointment of keeper Ian Andrews and centre-half Russell Osman.

Left: Graham Taylor's first spell as Villa boss might have been a highly successful time for the club but it didn't start on the brightest note. After a 1-1 draw at Ipswich in the former Watford manager's first match, his side lost 2-0 to Birmingham in their opening home game despite this emphatic punch by Nigel Spink. The no 4 for a side beaten at Hull next time out is Neale Cooper and the no 10 is David Hunt.

Below: John Gidman, a popular Villa man of the 1970s, looks on (left) as Martin Keown makes his presence felt in the Second Division home clash with Manchester City on August 31, 1987. Kevin Gage, one of several low-key summer signings by Graham Taylor, scored the goal but the 1-1 draw meant Villa hadn't won any of their first four League matches.

Moment of club history for Mark Walters as he scores Villa's 6,000th Football League goal. The strike was the only one of the game at home to Bournemouth on October 17, 1987 and meant Villa's promotion challenge was growing. They had gone eight League games without defeat and were emerging as a particular threat on their travels.

The goals flowed when Villa took on visiting Plymouth on February 27, 1988. With David Platt at the club after a £200,000 switch from Crewe, the prospect of an instant return to the top flight was increasing almost by the week. Nigel Spink saves well here but Villa ran amok to complete a high-scoring double over the Devonians via a 5-2 victory, sealed by goals from Paul Birch (2), Stuart Gray, Garry Thompson and Platt, the latter on his home debut.

A hiccup on the road to promotion as a chance eludes Garry Thompson in the 2-1 home defeat against Leeds on March 12, 1988. Alan McInally's goal wasn't enough to stave off a surprise loss following two successive victories but Villa bounced back well to win 2-0 at Reading in their next fixture - one of no fewer than 15 away wins they managed that season in League and cups.

Stuart Gray unsuccessfully tries to find a way through as Villa continue to suffer the promotion jitters at home to Oldham on April 4, 1988. The 2-1 defeat was the side's third consecutive odd-goal setback after beatings at the hands of Stoke and Millwall - and the road back to the big time was proving anything but easy to negotiate.

Tony Daley gets up close and personal with his marker in Villa's edgy 1-0 home win over Shrewsbury on April 23, 1988. The winger was hailed as one of the club's most exciting players for years when he burst on to the scene and played a good part in their return to health. Warren Aspinall, a useful legacy from the brief Billy McNeill era, was the match-winner - his 11th goal of the season.

Even a victory at Swindon in Villa's final game would have been insufficient to win promotion had Middlesbrough taken just a point at home to Leicester or if Bradford had beaten visiting Ipswich. But Boro, managed by former Villa favourite Bruce Rioch, and Bradford, who had lost 1-0 at Villa Park shortly before, were defeated, making Villa's 0-0 draw at the County Ground good enough to give them runners-up spot behind Millwall. Here, with the travelling masses ready to acclaim a vital goal, David Platt does his best to lift the unbearable tension but is frustrated by the bravery of keeper Fraser Digby.

More images of a tense final afternoon at Swindon's County Ground. Above: Anxious looks all round as, with their game finished, Villa's players and supporters wait for confirmation of what had happened elsewhere. And, below: The celebrations begin and the champagne comes out. Villa were promoted while Middlesbrough and Bradford were consigned to the play-offs, in which Boro prevailed.

Back Where They Belong

It looks like a David Platt goal on Villa's first day back in the top flight - but the scorer is Alan McInally, who can be seen turning towards the Witton Lane Stand in celebration of this strike against fellow new arrivals Millwall. A Stuart Gray penalty provided Villa's other goal in a 2-2 draw, McInally going on to net a further 17 times before Christmas, including a gem in the Littlewoods Cup against Millwall.

Villa lost 2-0 to Liverpool in a 1987-88 FA Cup tie but did better when the Merseysiders visited on September 10, 1988. Although David Platt goes close here for a side who had won 3-2 at Arsenal the previous weekend, it was no 9 Alan McInally who scored in a 1-1 draw - his fourth goal in three games. Also pictured are Allan Evans and Liverpool trio Bruce Grobbelaar, Ronnie Whelan and Gary Gillespie.

Derek Mountfield, a centre-half with a goal-scoring knack, beats Peter Shilton to net for the first time as a Villa player in the League game at home to Derby on November 19, 1988. The former Everton man, who once headed a crucial goal for the Toffees in an FA Cup semi-final at the ground, was to hit the target 17 times in 120 games for Villa, although this match ended in a second successive defeat.

Debutant Ian Ormondroyd takes evasive action as David Platt volleys a trademark goal to help Villa to a 2-0 home win over Sheffield Wednesday on February 4, 1989. Derek Mountfield looks on during a game in which Nigel Callaghan also made his first Villa appearance - and celebrated by scoring. Graham Taylor's side narrowly avoided the drop in their first season back in the elite.

Not a bad day's work! Graham Taylor shows off two new signings in 1989 - Dwight Yorke (right) and Colvin Hutchinson. The duo had been spotted during Villa's trip to Trinidad and Tobago earlier in the year and were brought to the UK with mixed results. Hutchinson did not make the grade but Yorke became a massive success in this country, at both Villa and Manchester United.

After their flirt with relegation, Villa started 1989-90 poorly as they drew three and lost one of their first four games. But this visit of Tottenham on September 9 broke the ice and Ian Olney, trying to get the better of Paul Gascoigne as David Platt challenges, scored both goals in a 2-0 win. Even with Paul McGrath now in their defence, Villa still lost their next two games before taking off spectacularly.

Graham Taylor, having reportedly gone close to the sack in the autumn of 1989, had his side on a real roll by the time they hammered Everton 6-2 in front of the live TV cameras on November 5. This was one of David Platt's two goals, flashed past ex-Villa man Martin Keown, with Ian Olney (2), Kent Nielsen and Gordon Cowans netting the others. Villa were on a run of eight wins in nine League games.

The sequence of success had stretched to ten victories in 13 First Division matches after Villa had seen off visiting Arsenal in this clash on December 30, 1989. Derek Mountfield scores here with a header and David Platt netted the other in a 2-1 victory. When Villa went top two days later by winning 3-0 at Chelsea, their supporters were even dreaming of the club lifting the League Championship again.

The title challenge continues to gather momentum! David Platt celebrates in front of the Holte End after obliging with the only goal of the clash with Big Ron's Sheffield Wednesday in early February, 1990. It was a 15th League goal of the season for Platt - and he emerged as Villa's top scorer prior to becoming a global star when he took his blistering form into the 1990 World Cup finals in Italy.

It wasn't just in the League that Villa made exciting progress in 1989-90. They also played no fewer than 14 ties in knockout football, including this (right) 2-0 FA Cup fifth-round victory at Albion, clinched by goals from Derek Mountfield and Tony Daley. Mountfield is in the thick of things here as he watches Paul McGrath and Ian Ormondroyd put paid to a Baggies attack. Chris Price is on the right.

Below: Ian Ormondroyd takes aim and fires through a cluster of players, including fellow scorer David Platt and Ian Olney, to give Villa the lead in their game at Tottenham on February 21, 1990. This 2-0 victory was as good as it got for Graham Taylor's men, a seventh successive League win leaving them clear at the top of the table. But they lost to Wimbledon and Coventry in their next two fixtures and the impetus was checked.

Villa were running almost on empty by the time they ground out this 1-0 home win over Chelsea on April 14, 1990. With Liverpool in firm control at the top, thoughts of the title had virtually gone and Second City sights were only on second place. Gordon Cowans is pictured here scoring the winner for a side who had won at Arsenal in their previous game but had lost their two matches before that.

Villa's last success of a tremendous campaign came here by a 1-0 scoreline at home to Millwall on April 21, 1990. David Platt scored the only goal at a time when striker Tony Cascarino (left) was still feeling his feet following his £1.5m move from The Den. Chris Price is the man on the ball for a team whose worst fears were realised a few weeks later when Graham Taylor left to succeed Bobby Robson as England boss after the World Cup finals in Italy.

The 1990-91 campaign dawned with Jozef Venglos holding the managerial reins at Villa Park - and the Czech's first game in charge brought a modest 1-1 home draw with Southampton. Tim Flowers takes the ball off the toe of Villa's goalscorer Tony Cascarino here, with Micky Adams (left) among the relieved Saints defenders. The club lost their next two League games and were to finish in a bitterly disappointing 17th place only 12 months after being runners-up to Liverpool.

Moment to remember for David Platt as he rounds off a move he had started and scores Villa's second goal in their UEFA Cup 2-0 home win over Inter Milan on October 24, 1990. Kent Nielsen had netted the first goal for a side who beat Banik Ostrava home and away in the previous round. Alas, Villa couldn't complete the job in the San Siro Stadium in the second leg and were beaten 3-0 in front of 75,580.

Legend at work....the imperious Paul McGrath holds off the familiar figure of Mark Walters in Villa's 4-2 home win over FA Cup holders Liverpool in September, 1992, the first season of the FA Premiership. McGrath had been signed three and a bit years earlier by Graham Taylor for £450,000 from Manchester United and played a full part as Villa made superb progress under Ron Atkinson and Jim Barron in 1992-93. Two goals by ex-Anfield star Dean Saunders set up this win, which came early in an unbeaten run of ten League games.

Contrasting images of Villa's spring of 1993. Above: The beaming smile of Dwight Yorke says it all in a 2-0 home victory over Sheffield Wednesday on March 20. It was the side's ninth win in 13 matches and kept them well in the running for the inaugural Premier League title. The impetus was maintained with maximum points at Nottingham Forest and Arsenal but Villa lost steam and were beaten in their final three games, the second of them (below) bringing disappointed looks as Paul McGrath left the field after a 1-0 Oldham win.

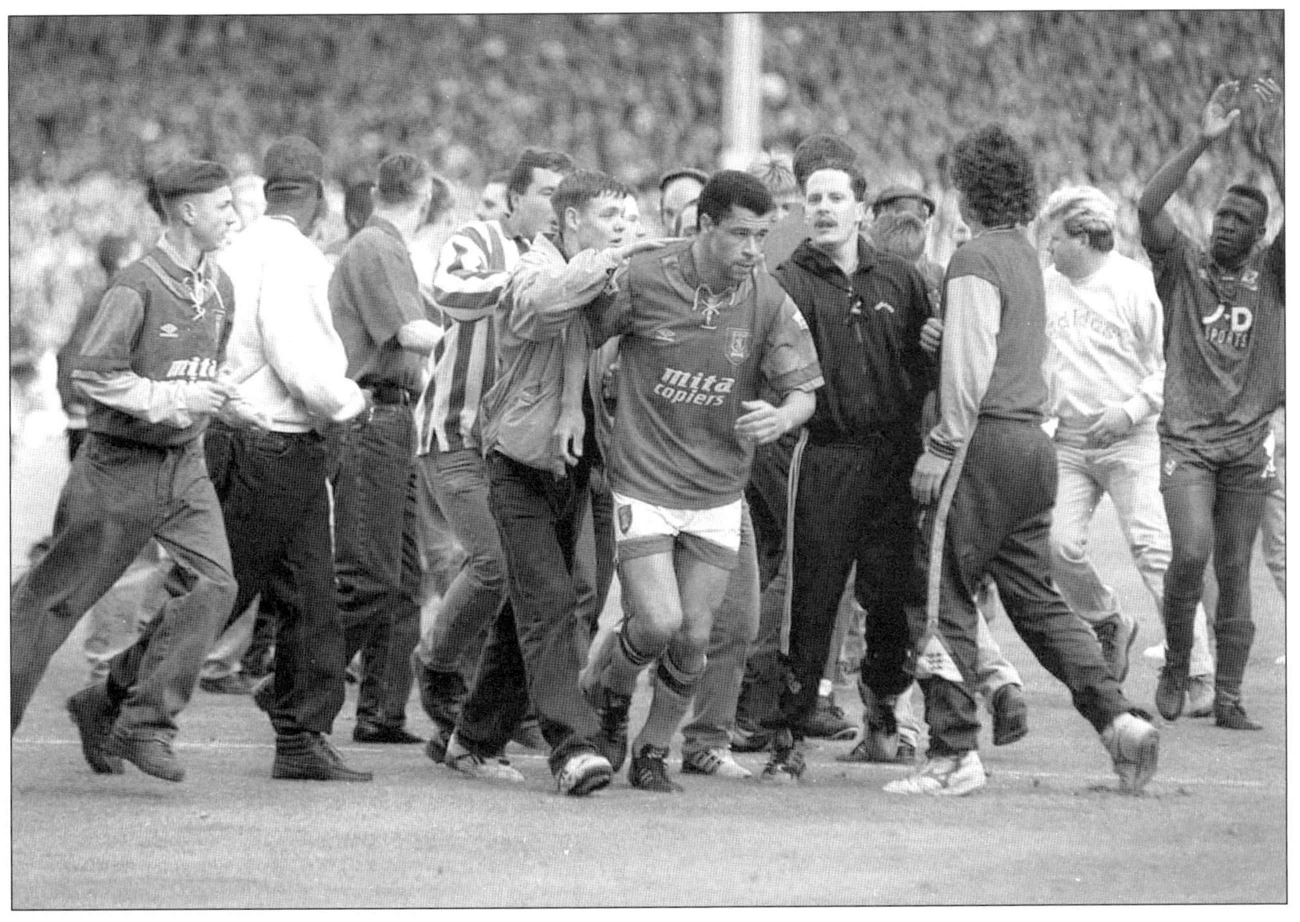

Steve Staunton acclaims his winner at home to Tottenham - the only goal of the game - at the start of an impressive run for the club in the opening weeks of 1993-94. Fellow defender Earl Barrett is the player about to heap his congratulations on a man who played exactly 350 competitive games in two spells with Villa, joining them for £1.1m in 1991 and on a free in 2000 after an absence of two and a half years. He also has more Republic of Ireland caps (102) than anyone.

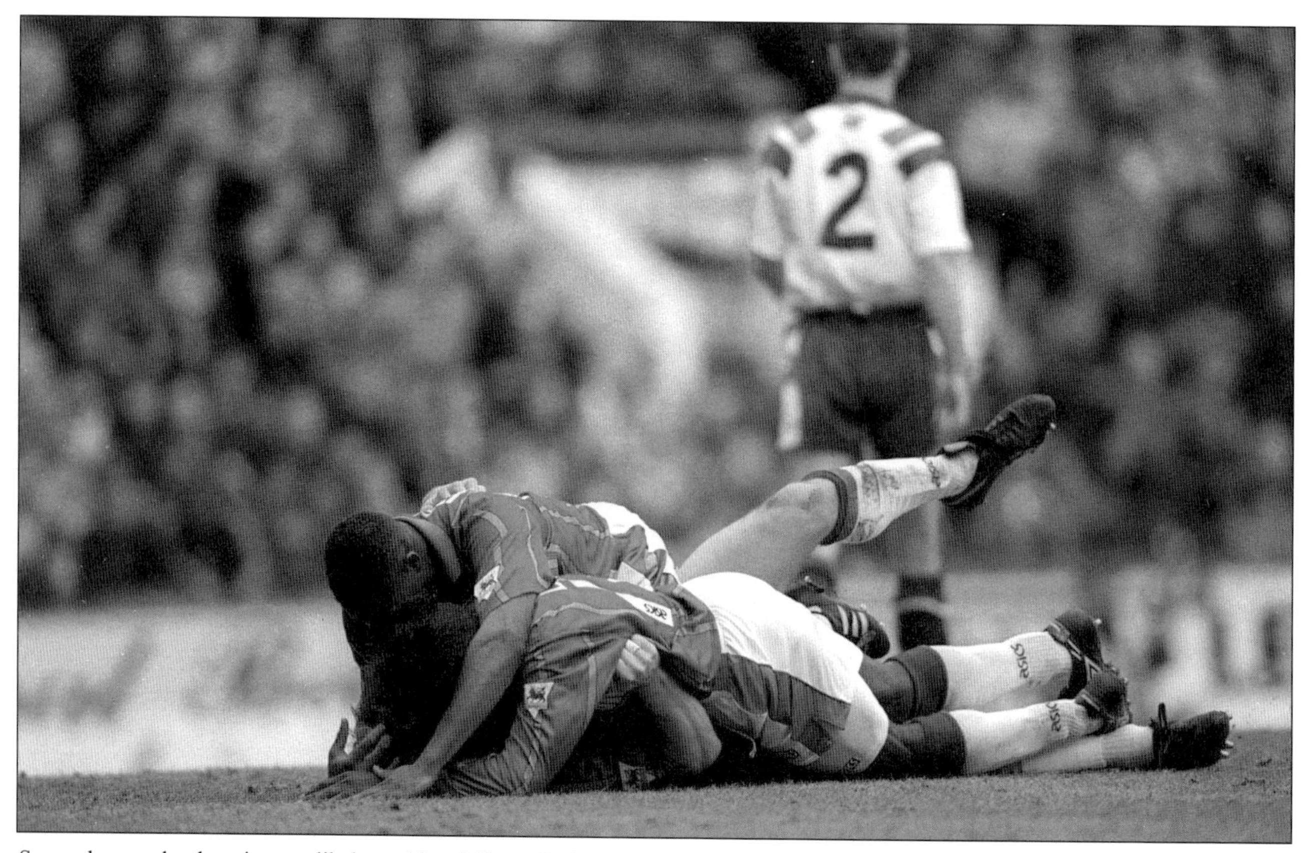

Somewhere under there is an unlikely goal hero! Shaun Teale, who scored only five times in 181 Villa games, came up with one of those 'strikes' just when his side needed it in their Coca-Cola Cup semi-final return against Tranmere on February 27, 1994. The Merseysiders led 3-1 from the first leg but were beaten by the same score at Villa Park before Ron Atkinson's men won the penalty shoot-out. Joining in with the celebrations here are Teale's fellow scorer Dalian Atkinson and Tony Daley. Dean Saunders netted the other goal.

Coca-Cola Fizz!

A nonchalant early finish from Dalian Atkinson - and Villa are one up mid-way through the first half of their Coca-Cola Cup final against hot favourites Manchester United. The trailing defenders are Steve Bruce (left) and Gary Pallister while the United keeper is former Villa man Les Sealey. In that pre-Beckham era, Sir Alex Ferguson also had the likes of Eric Cantona and Mark Hughes in his line-up.

More agony for United as Les Sealey is beaten by a Dean Saunders effort that squeezes inside his right-hand post for goal no 2. The bit of breathing space came with only a quarter of an hour left and started to convince Villa supporters that this was to be ***their*** day. Saunders' goal was a neat deflection to skipper Kevin Richardson's free-kick. The Villa player to the left is Shaun Teale, who played with a broken nose - an injury kept secret from the opposition following a training-ground collision with ex-United keeper Mark Bosnich.

Tony Daley, having hit the woodwork shortly before, cadges a lift as he congratulates Dean Saunders on scoring Villa's killer third goal. Saunders, deployed as a lone striker as Ron Atkinson used Dalian Atkinson in a five-man midfield, opted to go straight and true when netting from the penalty spot a minute from time following a handball to an Atkinson shot that saw Andrei Kanchelskis sent off. Mark Hughes had set up a tense finish by making it 2-1 in the 82nd minute.

Villa's ecstatic players toast their unlikely success in time-honoured fashion. Manchester United had been 7-2 on favourites as they chased a domestic treble - and underlined what a coup this was for Ron Atkinson's men by bouncing back to win the Premiership for the second year running and beat Chelsea 4-0 in the FA Cup final. For Big Ron, the Premiership's oldest manager at the age of 55, it was nothing new. It was his third time as a Wembley winner - with different clubs - having also plotted United's downfall as Sheffield Wednesday boss in the 1991 Rumbelows Cup final. From this happy group, Tony Daley and Steve Froggatt joined their former boss Graham Taylor at Wolves only a few weeks later.

COCA-COLA FIZZ!

What it's all about! Captain Kevin Richardson shows off the spoils of success - a shock triumph underlined by the fact his side had lost home and away to Manchester United in the League that season and lost to Ipswich, Leeds and Oldham in the three games immediately before Wembley. The inspirational midfielder also picked up the Alan Hardaker Trophy as man of the match in Villa's first final at the twin towers for 17 years. Victory meant they joined Nottingham Forest and Liverpool as the only clubs to win the competition four times.

Job done! Andy Townsend starts the celebrations after Villa made it back to Wembley on the away goals rule via a 0-0 second-leg draw with Arsenal in the 1996 Coca-Cola Cup semi-final. Townsend was inspirational in the captain's armband and made 176 appearances for the club to go with the 70 senior Republic of Ireland caps he won. In the background, a more muted Alan Wright shakes hands with Dennis Bergkamp.

Villa had not lost at Wembley in more than a quarter of a century when they set off for the twin towers for the Coca-Cola Cup final against Leeds on March 24, 1996. And Brian Little's side rarely looked like surrendering that proud record as they raced to a 3-0 victory, helped on their triumphant way by this terrific long-range strike by Savo Milosevic that the lunging John Pemberton was unable to cut out. On the right is Leeds skipper Gary McAllister.

Ian Taylor jogs away to milk the celebrations after scoring goal no 2 in one of Wembley's more one-sided finals. The loyal midfielder, a boyhood Villa fan, is pursued by Dwight Yorke, who netted a late third and was to end the season with a handsome haul of 25 goals. Defender David Wetherall sums up Leeds' despair by putting his head in his hands.

Let the party begin! Gareth Southgate and Ugo Ehiogu each get a hand on the silverware (above) as Villa celebrate equalling Liverpool's record as five-time League Cup winners. The two defenders both found the 1995-96 season notable at international level, too, Ehiogu making his England debut and Southgate achieving notoriety as the man who missed the crucial penalty against Germany in a shoot-out in the semi-final of the European Championships three months later.

Joy for John Gregory's Villa as Lee Hendrie and goalscorer Dwight Yorke celebrate in front of an ecstatic capacity crowd after the conversion of a cheeky penalty in the 1-0 victory at home to Arsenal on the last day of the 1997-98 season. The victory, the club's ninth in 11 matches under Gregory - Brian Little's successor as manager - was to prove enough to seal unlikely qualification for the UEFA Cup via a final League placing of seventh.

Dion Dublin hails Villa's fans after completing his hat-trick in the 4-1 win over Southampton at The Dell on November 14, 1998 - the day Villa set a club record 12 League games unbeaten at the start of a season. Dublin won the last of his four England caps four days later. Alas, they had already gone out of the UEFA Cup to Celta Vigo at the second hurdle despite winning the away first leg.

Benito Carbone, a genial Italian who had already made his name in English football with Sheffield Wednesday, goes into shirt-waving mode after completing a stunning hat-trick against Leeds in the fifth round of the FA Cup on January 30, 2000. George Boateng is in hot pursuit of a player whose heroics in an exhilerating 3-2 Villa Park victory, included a goal of the season effort. Carbone scored in the next round as well at Everton, where he was also sent off in a 2-1 win.

Paul Merson salutes Villa's celebrating supporters after the wearing down of Second Division Bolton in the FA Cup semi-final amid the unusual surroundings of Wembley in April, 2000. The underdogs gave every bit as good as they got in the 120 minutes of normal time and extra time and Villa were relieved to sneak through to their first FA Cup final for 43 years thanks to Dion Dublin's winning kick in the penalty shoot-out. Merson scored 19 goals in 145 appearances for the club after being signed by John Gregory for £6.75m from Middlesbrough.

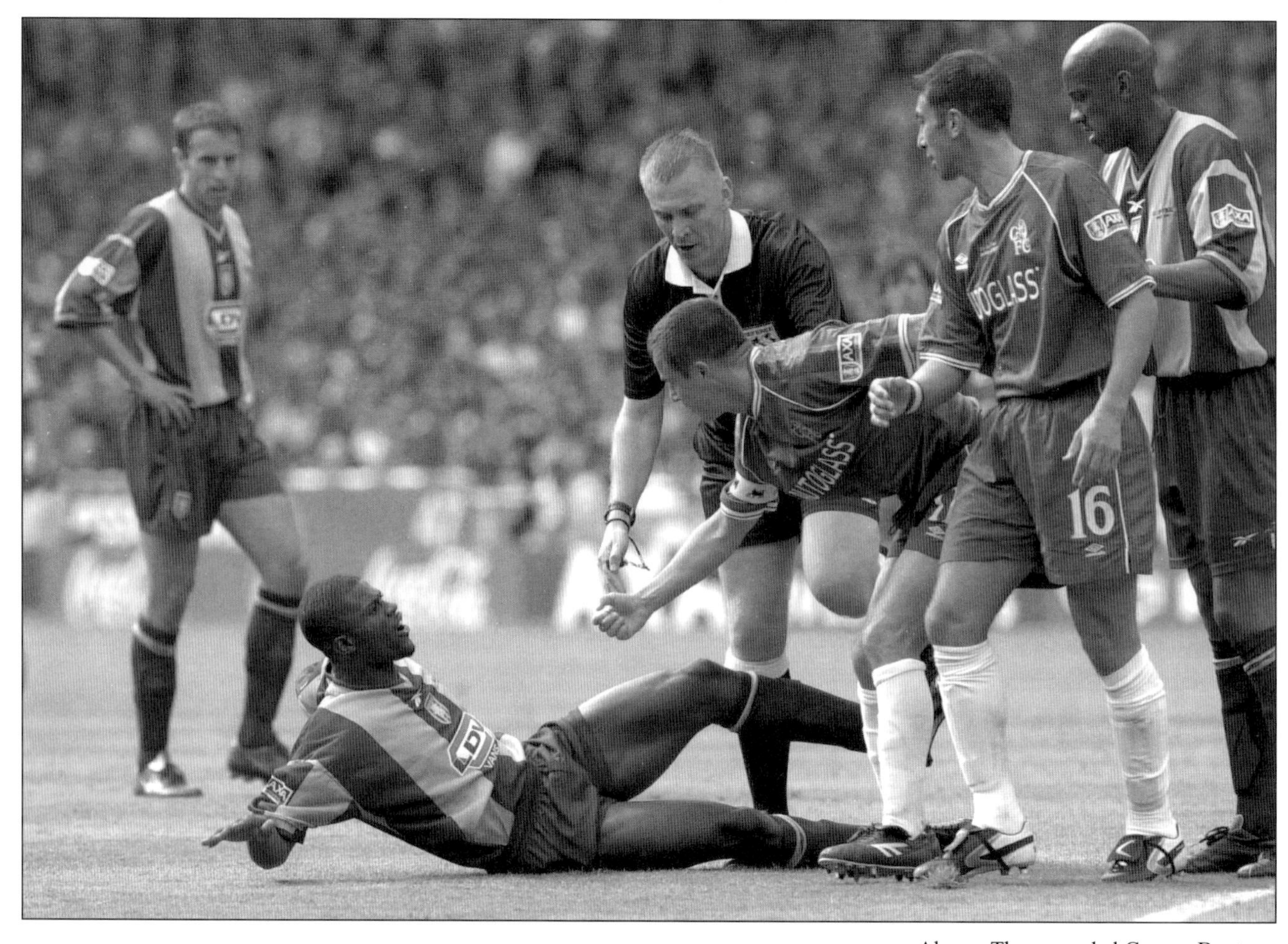

Above: The grounded George Boateng finds himself on the end of some typical Dennis Wise verbals in Villa's disappointing FA Cup final defeat by Chelsea in May, 2000. The only goal came from Roberto Di Matteo, who is seen here on the fringe of things with Dion Dublin and Gareth Southgate.

Bloodied but unbowed - Olof Mellberg leaves the field after Villa had gallantly failed to pull back Bolton's 5-2 first-leg lead in the Carling Cup semi-final of 2003-04. Villa won 2-0 on the evening and so went out - but not before a show of the spirit that can lead them to more heights in the future.

Subscribers

SCROLL OF HONOUR

David Allcote
B R G Andrew
Kevin Andrews
Keith Arnold
Alex Ashford
Robert Ashman
Mart, Deb, Nik, and Ris Attwood

Heath Baker
David T Barlow
Damian Barrow
Garry Bartlett
Arthur Bent
Alex, Dan and Paul Berwick
Peter John Bird
Neil S Black
Terry Blundell
Terry Boland
Kris Bolton
Matthew J Boss
Michael Thomas Bourne
Kerry Boyd
Ben Bradburn
David Breeze
David and Pam Bridgewater
Clare Cheryl Briggs
John Briggs
Trevor James Broadbent
Jim Brolan
Benjamin Brooke
Russell John Broomhall
Matthew Brough
Lawson Bullivant
John Edward Butler
Jez and Drew Byrne

Gavin Callow
Andy Campkin (Aylesbury)
Ian David Carpenter
Dean Adam Carter
Mark Cheek
David Clayton
Ashley Robert Coley
Andrew Collins
Anthony Conaghan
Tom, Kieran, and Kerry Conway
Andrew John Cooper
Malcolm Cooper
Stephen Corcoran
Gary Costello
Sean Costello
David F Cox
Paul Crane
Terry Curley

Alf Dale
Andrew Dale
Jim Dale

SCROLL OF HONOUR

Paul Darlington
Kenneth Davies
Marc and Angela Davies
Paul Davies
Mike Davis
Lionel Deeley
Jim and Mandy Delaney
Jon Dench
H John Desaulles
John Devenney
Carl Matthew Dodd
Greg Dollery
Pete Doolan
Michael Dorans
Clive John Doyle
Steve Drew
Clifford Paul Dubberley

David, Susan and Oliver Eagle
Paul Edmonds (Blackpool)
Leigh Edwards
Michael S Edwards
Norman Edwards
Paul Edwards
Rob Edwards
Joanne Elford
Martin Elmslie
Jack Edward Elwell and Grandad
C R Evans

Andrew Geoffrey Field
Alexander Flavell
Thomas Andrew Forbes (Forbsey)
Paul Ford
John Foster
Gerry Furness

Paul Gamwell
Neil Gardner (Holte End)
Allan Garrish
Nigel Garrity
Maurice Gavin
Kevin Gledhill
Lucien Goddard
Robert Gough
John A Gould (1934)
Erroll Grant
Ian and Helen Gray (Chatteris)
Philip Gray
Gavin Green
Mark Stuart Green
Alex Groemminger
Guinness John Royal Mail

Barry Haggitt
William L Hales (since 1945)
Nigel Hamilton
Mark Harris and Ted Smith
Harris Villans (Bridgnorth)

SCROLL OF HONOUR

Steve Hawker
Mark Hazel
Robert William Head
Lee Henry
David Hodges (Southam)
Trevor Alan Holloway
Mark Homer (H)
Andrew D Horton
David Horton
Matthew Houlden
Ray Hourihan
Ole Hove
Peter Howard
David Howarth
George Howarth
Martin H Hughes 1971-2004
Peter L Hughes Jnr
Albert L Hughes 1906-1956
Peter L Hughes Snr
Adrian Spencer Humphries
Luke Hurley

David Patrick Jackson
Peter Jackson
Stephen James
Conner Jones
Gareth C Jones (Bones)
Neil Jones (Holte End)
Paul A Jones

Leyton Jordan
Wendy Jordan

Jack, Ester, Paul and Jenny Kirby
Jon, Pauline and Thomas Knibb
Andrew Knowles
Anthony Koumi

David Graham Lane
John Lane
Kevin Larkin
Michael John Leahy
John Lee

Scott MacKenzie
Carol Mannion in loving memory of
Dennis Mannion
Kenneth J Marriott
Bill Marron
Paul Martin
Tony Mason (ex Erdington)
David McCranor
Warren, Ellie and Harry McDivitt
Kevin McGovern
Dennis and Julie McNamee
Steven Medlicott
Andrew Micklewright
Sophie May Millard
Andrew Moseley

SCROLL OF HONOUR

Simon Moseley
Helen Mullooly
Kevin P Mulrey
C Mynard

Charles Raymond Nelson
Desmond Nevin

Wayne O'Neill

Anthony Roy Pash
Alan Michael Paton
David Peacock
Connor Lee Phillips
John Phipps
Russell Potter
In memory of Steven Powell
John (Villa) Power
William Powers
Nick and Ryan Pratt
Susan Pudge
Richard Pursehouse

Sharaze Rahaman
John Rake
Stewart Leonard Ratcliff
John Edwin Raven
Bill Rawbone
Ian James Reed

Nigel and Lynda Renshaw
Steve and Elaine Renshaw
John Richmond
Gary Rigby
Adam Matthew Roberts
Michael Robertson
Abbi Rodgers
Daniel James Rowland

Martin Sanders
Richard Sandiford
Barry and Mark Santy
Julie Schladitz
Brian C Seadon
Keith Roger Shaw
Lee and Alex Shellum
John Shilcof
Russell Simpson
Daniel (Smudger) Smith
Dave Smith (VTID and on)
Jonathan (Jono) Smith
Martin Robert Smith
Bill Smyth
Holte Snelson 19/6/05
Robert Southall
George Southall-Brown
Jamie Sparrow
Martin Spencer
Mel Sperry

Scroll of Honour

Derrick Spinks
Andrew Sproston
Colin Sproston
Darren Sproston
David Sproston
Mark Sproston
Richard Sproston
Brett Stevens
Peter Stokes
Richard Stokes

Joseph Tassell
Malcolm Taylor
Richard Thacker
M C Thomas
Sue and Mick Tilt
Darren Tocker
David Treadwell
Kevin W Tromans

Steven Vickers

R N and D J Waters
Alan and Craig Watson (Dumfries)
Gary Weaver
Russell Paul Weir
Philip Clive Wharton
Graham M Wheeler
Alan James Whelan
Christopher J Whitaker
Andrew Whitehead
Lee Williams
Paul G Williams
Graham Willis
Ralph Willis (Middlesbrough)
Christian Wilson
Derek Wisdom
Roger Wooldridge
Anthony Woolley
Christopher Wormall
Adam John Wright

Steven John Yeomans
Stuart Ryan Yeomans
Wayne York

Other titles by Thomas Publications

(All written by David Instone unless otherwise stated)

The Bully Years (£8.99)

Wolves: Exclusive! (£6.99)

Sir Jack (£12.99)

Forever Wolves (£16.99)

When We Won the Cup (£15.99)

Running With Wolves by Peter Lansley (£16.99)

Le Tissier by Jeremy Butler (£14.99)

Wolves: The Glory Years (£16.99)

All these books are available by writing to:
Thomas Publications
PO Box 17
Newport
Shropshire
TF10 7WT

by phoning:
07734 440095

or by emailing:
info@thomaspublications.co.uk.

Further information about all of the above titles can be obtained by logging on to our website: www.thomaspublications.co.uk.